WITHDRAWN
UTSA LIBRARIES

Change and Tradition
Cultural and Historical Perspectives

The World of Christopher Columbus Imperial Spain 1469-1598

Emma Lou Thornbrough
BUTLER UNIVERSITY

Copley Publishing Group
Acton, Massachusetts 01720

Copyright © 1997 by Emma Lou Thornbrough
All rights reserved
Printed in the United States of America

ISBN 0-87411-919-7

Permission in writing must be obtained from the publisher before any part of this work may be reproduced or transmitted in any form or by any means, electronic or mechanical, including photocopying and recording, or by any information storage or retrieval system.

CONTENTS

CHRONOLOGICAL TABLE — v
INTRODUCTION — vii

PART I

GEOGRAPHY AND HISTORY — 3
  The Land and People — 3
A HISTORICAL SURVEY OF SPAIN TO 1469 — 9
  Romans and Visigoths — 9
  Muslim Spain — 12
  The Christian States and the
    Beginnings of the Reconquest — 17

PART II

THE SPAIN OF FERDINAND AND ISABELLA — 23
  The Catholic Monarchs — 23
  Society and Social Classes — 31
  Religion and the Church — 43

PART III

THE WORLD COLUMBUS DISCOVERED:
  SPAIN'S BEGINNINGS IN AMERICA — 55
  Beginnings of Settlement and Cultural Exchange — 59
  Spaniards and Native Americans — 64
  Government and Society in the Colonies — 70

PART IV

SPAIN UNDER THE EARLY HABSBURGS	81
Charles V and Philip II	81
Foreign Policies and Wars	86
Economy and Finance	94
The Golden Century	101

CONCLUSION

AFTERMATH AND LEGACY	111
WORKS CITED	115

MAPS

SPAIN IN 1500	5
MESO-AMERICA IN THE AGE OF THE CONQUISTADORS	57
EUROPE 1516–1598	83

CHRONOLOGICAL TABLE

206 B.C.–409 A.D.	Roman Spain
414	Visigoths invade Spain
456	Visigothic Kingdom
711	Visigoths defeated by invading Muslims
929-1031	Golden Age of Caliphate at Córdoba
1085	Toledo recaptured by Christians
1146	Almohads invade Spain
1212	Victory of Christian armies at Battle of Toledo
1236	Córdoba reconquered
c. 1243	Salamanca University
1248	Seville reconquered
1453	Constantinople captured by Ottoman Turks
1469	Marriage of Ferdinand and Isabella
1474	Isabella Queen of Castile
1480	Spanish Inquisition established
1492	Surrender of Granada—Reconquest completed
1492	Expulsion of Jews
1492	First voyage of Columbus to America
1493	First permanent settlement on Hispaniola
1494	Treaty of Tordesillas
1498	Santo Domingo, first city founded in New World
1502	Muslims in Spain given choice of conversion to Christianity or expulsion

1515–1582	St. Teresa of Ávila
1516–1555	Reign of Charles V (Carlos I)
1519–1522	Conquest of Mexico by Cortés
1521	Martin Luther excommunicated
1531–1534	Conquest of Peru by Pizarro
1539	Society of Jesus founded by Loyola
1545–1563	Council of Trent
1547–1616	Miguel de Cervantes
c. 1548–1614	El Greco
1551	University of Mexico
1555	Diet of Augsburg—recognition of Protestant princes of Germany
1555–1598	Reign of Philip II
1561	Madrid made capital of Spain
1571	Battle of Lepanto
1576	Sack of Antwerp
1580	Portugal annexed to Spain
1588	Invincible Armada defeated
1599–1660	Velasquez
1600–1681	Calderón de la Barca
1605	First part of *Don Quixote* published
1609–1611	Expulsion of Moriscos by Philip III
1648	Treaty of Westphalia—Netherlands independent
1700–1746	Reign of Philip V, first Bourbon King of Spain

INTRODUCTION

Most Americans associate the names of Ferdinand and Isabella, the rulers of Spain, with Christopher Columbus, whose voyage of "discovery" of America was made under the authority of Queen Isabella. Indeed, in sponsoring the voyages of Columbus the Spanish monarchs played a part in ushering in a new era. The voyages and the exploration and conquests which followed were a turning point in history, beginning the transmission of European institutions and culture to the Western Hemisphere, a development which would transform the Old World and the New. Since earliest times the Mediterranean had been the center of commerce and mingling of civilizations. Now the Atlantic Ocean would become a thoroughfare for commerce and movement of peoples and cultures.

In this era of rapid and dynamic change Spain took the lead. In a few years *conquistadores* (conquerors) had discovered, conquered, and imposed her rule over a vast domain. The Spanish Empire, the first great colonial empire, was firmly established a century before England and France had begun exploration and settlement in the Americas. The silver mines in Mexico and Peru brought unprecedented wealth, helping Spain to become for a time the most powerful state in Europe. In the wake of the *conquistadores,* missionaries and settlers brought the Spanish language and institutions to the New World and converted a large native population to the Roman Catholic religion. In consequence of Spanish colonization a Hispanic-American culture prevails in much of the western hemisphere today. We cannot understand this Spanish legacy in America without some knowledge of the history and institutions of the Spain from which it came.

The focus of our study will be Spain in the period 1469–1598. We begin with the marriage of Ferdinand and Isabella, which united the kingdoms of Aragon and Castile, and was an important step in the political unification of Spain. During their reign, the surrender of Granada in 1492 completed the Christian Reconquest from the Muslims who had invaded Spain more than seven hundred years before. Henceforth a primary objective of Spanish rulers was to preserve Spain as a Christian state, a bastion of the Roman Catholic Church. For Ferdinand and Isabella, "The Catholic Monarchs," the unity and strength of Spain depended on religious unity.

Under their successors, Charles V and Philip II, Spain reached the apex of her power and prestige in Europe. Wealth from the New World was used to beautify Spain and to maintain her military power. This was "The Golden Century," when Spain was a center of learning and of magnificent architecture. It was the greatest period in Spanish art and literature —the era of the painter El Greco and of Miguel de Cervantes, whose novel *Don Quixote* reflects the society of the age.

With both Charles and Philip foreign affairs and wars took precedence over internal matters in Spain. As Holy Roman Emperor as well as King of Spain, Charles spent much of his reign outside his Spanish realms. His son Philip was ruler of the Netherlands as well as the Spanish Empire. In the Mediterranean both kings faced the expanding power of the Ottoman Turks, a Muslim people. In northern Europe they were confronted with the rise of Protestantism, which was to shatter the unity of Roman Catholic Christendom. Both rulers used the resources and military and naval power of Spain to check the spread of Muslim power and in failed attempts to suppress the Protestant Revolt in Germany and the Netherlands.

We end our survey with the death of Philip II in 1598. By that time the decline of Spain from her dominant position in Europe had already begun. The self-confidence and dynamism of the age of discovery and conquest were replaced by discouragement and pessimism. Abroad Spain's military and naval forces had suffered reversals and humiliating defeats. At

Introduction

home the successors of Charles and Philip faced a staggering national debt and weakened economy.

The history of Spain in this era (1469–1598) is full of paradoxes and puzzles. In the New World Spain brought fundamental, sometimes ruthless change, while remaining at the same time the most tradition-bound of all western European societies. Why this paradox? Why was the age of Spain's greatness and pre-eminence in Europe so short? Why did the wealth from the mines of the New World not bring a strong economy and lasting prosperity to Spain? Perhaps learning more about the Spanish people and their rulers, about their society and institutions, will suggest some possible answers to these questions.

PART I

GEOGRAPHY AND HISTORY

The Land and the People

"To sixteenth century observers," writes a modern historian, "the most striking aspect of the Spanish landscape was its emptiness.... It was no coincidence that Don Quixote and Sancho travelled most of the time in solitude along deserted routes" (Lynch, 109). If aerial photography had existed in 1500 pictures of the area we call Spain would have shown a land of plateaus and plains surrounded and criss-crossed by mountains, snow capped in a few places. From the air the plateaus and plains would appear arid and barren, only sparsely cultivated with few signs of human habitation. But while travellers commented on the rugged mountains and large areas of arid uncultivated land, Spain was and is a land of geographical variety and contrasts.

The idea of Spain as a unified geographical entity covering the entire Iberian Peninsula goes back to the Romans, who called it Hispania. (Today modern Spain occupies about 85 percent of the Iberian Peninsula, Portugal the remainder.) But although the idea of Spain in this sense persisted, a united Iberia has never existed. Geography, as well as external forces, has been and continues to be an obstacle to unity.

The Iberian Peninsula, the most western of the peninsulas which thrust into the Mediterranean Sea from the north, is almost an island, surrounded by water except in the north, where the Pyrenees Mountains shut it off from the rest of the European continent. To the east is the Mediterranean; to the west the Atlantic Ocean. Portugal occupies a strip of land along the western coast, but Spain fronts on the Atlantic in the northwest and southwest. The narrow Straits of Gibraltar separate Spain from the north coast of Africa, and the proximity of Africa has led to movement of people across the straits throughout history, while geographical isolation from the rest of Europe has contributed to the distinctiveness of Spanish culture.

Mountain ranges divide Spain internally into a number of distinct regions. A large plateau, the *meseta*, occupies the central area, averaging about two thousand feet in height and surrounded by mountains. North of the *meseta* between Spain and France and extending westward is a rugged mountainous area. The extreme northwest coastal area, Galicia and Asturias, is a region of heavy rainfall with deciduous forests and green pasture lands, in contrast to the arid plateaus which cover most of the country. South of the *meseta* is Andalusia, stretching to the coast of the Mediterranean, a land of sub-tropical temperature and varied terrain. On the east coast, sloping from the interior mountains, are Aragon, Catalonia, and Valencia. Mountains and internal geography produced particularism and strong feelings of regional identity.

Spain is located in the temperate zone, but geographical conditions, altitude in particular, produce some extremes of temperature. The central plateaus experience scorching heat in summer and bitter cold in winter. Seasons of drought and rainfall alternate in most regions. In general Spain receives less rainfall than the rest of Europe, and some regions in the high central plateau receive little rain at any season. By contrast, the coastal plains in the east and south are very fertile where irrigation is available. Here are vineyards, orchards of olives, oranges, and other fruits, and rice fields.

Most rivers are deep, fast flowing, and comparatively short, seldom suitable for navigation. The longest river, the Tagus (*Tajo*), which winds its way across Spain, empties into the Atlantic in Portugal, as does the Duero in the north. The Guadalquivir flows into the Atlantic in southern Spain. Near its mouth is Seville, the port through which all trade with America

Geography and History

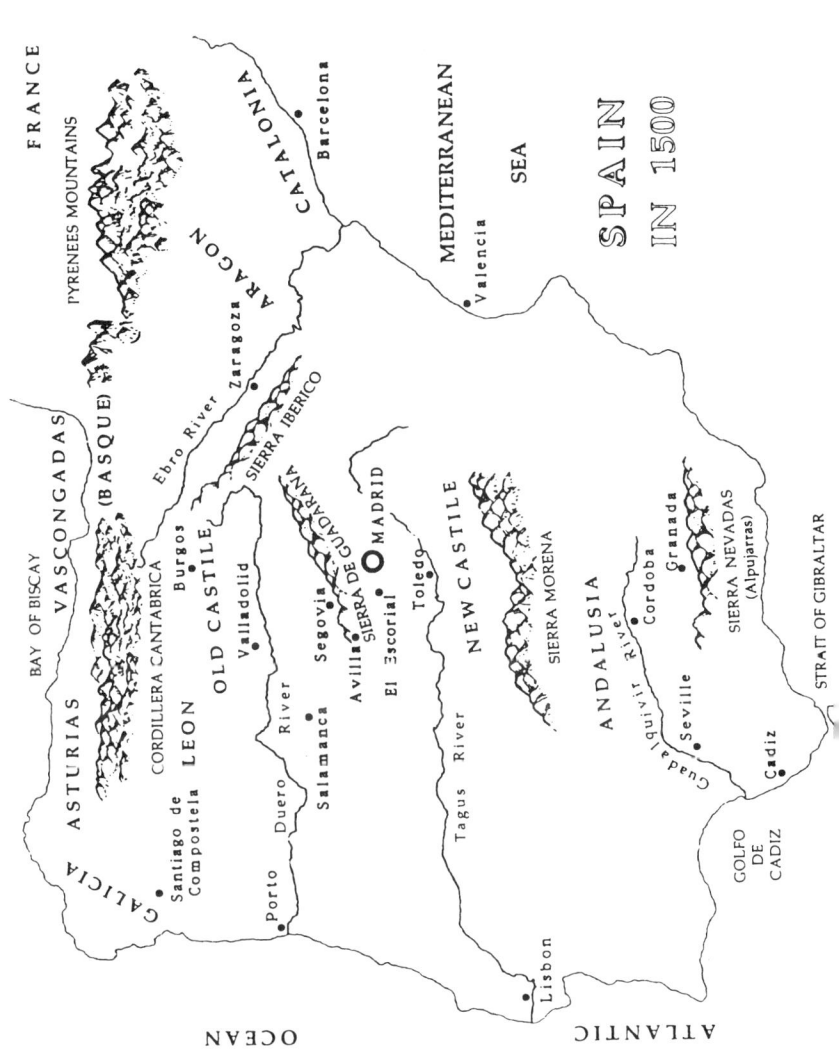

Map 1: Spain in 1500

passed. In the east the most important river is the Ebro, flowing through a fertile area of irrigated fields and orchards.

The Spanish of early modern times were a people of mixed ancestry, descendants of many groups who had invaded the peninsula over the centuries. The first people of whom there are records were known as Iberians. In the northwest were Celtic invaders, and in the central area a Celtic-Iberian population. Very early Phoenicians from Tyre (in modern Lebanon) founded colonies at modern Cadiz and other points. These were later taken over by Carthaginians, themselves descendants of Phoenicians. As Greeks explored and traded in the western Mediterranean they founded settlements along the east coast. Later Spain was conquered and incorporated into the Roman Empire. After the Romans came Germanic tribes, most important of whom were the Visigoths. In the eighth century Muslim invaders, Arabs and Berbers from North Africa, overran much of the peninsula.

This tradition of invasion and ethnic mixing had a dual impact in the period we are studying. During the fifteenth century Spanish Christians completed their "reconquest" of the Iberian peninsula from the Muslims. In many ways Spanish exploration and settlement of the New World can be seen as an extension of that "reconquest." Similarly, the ethnic mixing that occurred in Spain over the course of centuries made Spanish explorers more racially tolerant than other European colonizers. Thus one saw more intermarriage between Spaniards and natives than was the case for English and French settlers in the New World.

During the period of Rome's domination Latin became the official language of Hispania, and a kind of Latin became the spoken language of the people. Modern Spanish, a Romance language, developed from a mixture of the Latin of literature and the vulgar Latin spoken by Roman soldiers and traders, along with some Iberian and Celtic elements. Later Arabic words were incorporated. Geographic divisions fostered the development of many regional and local dialects. As Castile became politically dominant the language of that kingdom became the language of Spanish literature. Castilian was declared the official language of government, replacing Latin, by Emperor Charles V (Carlos I of Spain) in 1536.

A HISTORICAL SURVEY OF SPAIN TO 1469

Romans and Visigoths

The Spain of Ferdinand and Isabella was an amalgam of peoples, the descendants of invaders who arrived over many centuries, leaving their imprint on institutions and culture. No legacy was more important and lasting than that of Rome.

The Roman presence in Spain dated from the Second Punic War, at the end of which (206 B.C.) Carthage ceded her holdings in Spain to Rome. Eastern and southern regions submitted readily, but tribes in the mountainous interior tested Rome's best armies for generations and were not finally subdued until the time of Augustus. Meanwhile much of Spain, beginning with Andalusia in the south, became thoroughly Romanized. Throughout the peninsula cities captured or founded by Rome were centers of Roman government and administration and also Roman architecture and culture. Citizenship was granted early in the Roman period to most inhabitants.

The interior and rural districts took on a Roman character more slowly. As in other parts of the empire Roman military camps developed into Roman towns and cities. (For example, Saragossa was originally a camp, Caesaria Augusta.) Colonies formed in Spain by veterans of Roman armies contributed to the process of Romanization. But the extent of Rome's influence varied, the northern parts being least affected. The Basque people retained their tribal organization and their language.

By the time of Julius Caesar Latin had become the language of cultivated Iberians, and in the following centuries a Hispanicized Latin became the spoken language of most of the people. Roman law and administration had a lasting influence on later Spanish institutions.

Roman rule brought internal order, and, for a long time, security from external aggression. Hispania was important for a number of agricultural products, but it was the silver mines in the north that yielded the greatest wealth. Commerce flourished. A network of Roman roads, built originally for military purposes, facilitated internal trade and travel. Parts of the roads and the bridges which spanned them survive to the present, as do remnants of magnificent Roman aqueducts. The cities of Spain were among the largest and wealthiest of the Roman Empire. They were adorned by typical Roman buildings — basilicas, baths, theaters, and amphitheaters. Private residences ranged from multi-storied tenements to luxurious town houses and palaces. Roman type villas and farmhouses could be found in the countryside.

From Spain came the first Roman emperors of non-Italian stock, the great emperors of the second century, Trajan and Hadrian, who took with them to Rome many Spanish advisers and administrators. Theodosius, the emperor who established Christianity as the official religion, was also of Spanish origin. Many generals, jurists, and administrators from Spain served throughout the empire, and Spain was an important source of manpower for the Roman armies.

A number of writers and scholars of the "silver age" of Latin literature were Spanish. Among them were the Senecas, the elder and younger, Lucan, Martial, and Quintilian.

The most important and lasting Roman contribution to Spain was the establishment of the Christian religion. The origins of Christianity in the peninsula are obscure, but the new faith was probably introduced very early. (St. Paul mentioned his plan to visit Spain in his Letter to the Romans.) There is little evidence from the third century, but by the fourth century the names of a number of influential Spanish bishops are known. There was apparently a large number of Christians by 378 when Emperor Theodosius proscribed paganism and made Christianity the only tolerated religion.

A Historical Survey of Spain to 1469

In the late third and fourth centuries Spain suffered, as did much of the Roman Empire, from a decline in population, partly the result of plagues and epidemics and also of an increasingly oppressive government. As the power of Rome disintegrated during the later years of the empire, increasing numbers of Germanic "barbarians" invaded or infiltrated the border provinces. These invaders were sometimes destructive, but at other times their presence was welcomed by the inhabitants as a release from the oppression of the decaying empire. After several earlier waves of invaders a Germanic people, the Visigoths (western Goths), established a regime which controlled most of the Iberian Peninsula until the Muslim conquest in the eighth century.

The arrival of the Visigoths, who dominated the peninsula for three centuries, did not mark as sharp a break with the Roman past as might have been expected. One of the many Germanic tribes to invade the Roman Empire, they first arrived in the fourth century in the area around the Black Sea. Later they invaded Italy and carried out a sack of Rome itself in 410, but did not remain. Thereafter they established themselves in southern France and then moved into Spain. In 456 they proclaimed a Visigothic kingdom independent of Rome. Visigothic kings continued to rule until the Muslim conquest of Spain in the eighth century, but their kingdom was frequently torn by internal strife and fighting between rival claimants to the throne.

By the time they established themselves in Spain the Visigoths had had long contact with Rome and Roman institutions; their leaders had acquired some knowledge of Roman law and government and a veneer of Roman culture. On the whole they did not try to destroy Hispano-Roman civilization but to absorb and perpetuate it. Visigothic kings continued to work within the framework of institutions established under Rome.

Christianity and the Roman Catholic Church continued and in some ways grew stronger in this era. The Visigoths had already been exposed to Christianity before they arrived in

Spain. The rulers and their followers had been converted and baptized, but as Arian Christians, a group that had been declared heretical at the Council of Nicaea (325). Prior to their arrival the Spanish people had already become adherents of the orthodox Christianity of the Roman Church. At first there was friction between the two Christian factions, but later Visigoth kings, in an effort to strengthen unity, accepted the Nicene Creed. The kings exercised great power in church affairs, as kings were to do in the later history of Spain, but the prestige of the clergy, the most learned men of the time, was very great. By far the most important of them was Saint Isidore of Seville, author of numerous works of history, including a history of the Visigoths. The earliest monasteries in Spain had probably been founded during the Roman period, but their numbers and importance grew under the Visigoths. Probably the most enduring legacy of the Visigothic period was a powerful church and thoroughly Christianized populace.

Muslim Spain

The rise of a new religion, Islam, and the conquest by its followers of an empire stretching from the Pyrenees in the west to India in the east, all in a period of less than two hundred years, changed the course of history as have few developments. Spain was the westernmost part of the vast Islamic empire and the only part of it which was eventually restored to Christianity. Nevertheless the centuries of Muslim domination and the long struggle of the Christian Reconquest were of lasting influence in shaping the Spanish nation and the character of the Spanish people.

In 711 an army of perhaps twelve thousand crossed the narrow straits, less than ten miles wide, which separate Spain from Africa. They were a motley group—Arabs (mainly Syrians), Berbers from North Africa, and others of uncertain origin who had joined the ranks of the Muslims as they advanced across North Africa. The name of the Berber commander, Tarik, is preserved in the name Gibraltar, which translated from Arabic means Mount of Tarik. The invaders were immediately

A Historical Survey of Spain to 1469

victorious in a decisive battle in which the Visigoth king was apparently killed. Thereafter the confused and demoralized Visigoths were unable to consolidate their forces against the Muslims. In fact there is reason to believe that dissident elements in Spain may have welcomed the Muslim invaders and eased their conquest. After the first battle more reinforcements arrived from Africa. The advancing Muslim army laid siege to some towns, but in others encountered little resistance. By 718 Muslims were in control of the entire Iberian Peninsula, except for a few mountainous areas in the extreme north.

To understand the Muslim regime in Spain it will be helpful to make a brief survey of the nature of Islam and the Islamic conquests. The term Islam means "submission" (i.e. to God), and the name Muslim means "one who has submitted." The founder, the prophet Muhammad, was a caravan driver in western Arabia, a sparsely populated land of nomadic tribes, without any national consciousness. About 610 Muhammad began to receive revelations from God calling him to preach monotheism—that there was only one God—to his fellow Arabs. In addition certain ethical doctrines were revealed to him as well as injunctions about social behavior and law. The religion which he began to preach, based in part on the Jewish and Christian creeds, was one of great simplicity of doctrine. Muhammad regarded himself as a successor to Abraham, Moses, and Jesus and was so regarded by his followers. Islam required absolute submission to the will of God, a life of moral rectitude, prayers, fasting, and, if possible, a pilgrimage to the sacred city of Mecca. For the faithful a paradise of luxury and pleasures was promised; for others damnation in hell.

The holy book, Qur'an, which was revealed to Muhammad, contained in addition to religious doctrine guidance for all phases of the lives of the faithful—marriage and divorce, business, crime and punishment, peace and war. Under Islam there was no separation between the secular and religious life. The *Sharia* or Holy Law became the law of the land throughout the Muslim world.

By the time of his death Muhammad had converted most of his fellow Arabs and organized a theocratic state. His teaching and the requirements of the new religion had begun to organize nomadic tribes into a state. After his death a caliph (deputy or successor) was named as the supreme religious and political commander of Islam.

During Muhammad's lifetime his followers engaged in pillaging caravans of persons who rejected the new religion. After his death these raids developed into campaigns of conquest of non-Arab lands. With incredible speed the Persian Empire and a large portion of the Byzantine Empire were invaded and brought under Muslim rule. After routing a Byzantine army in Syria the Muslim armies quickly swept over the great cities of Antioch, Damascus, and Jerusalem, but they were unable to take Constantinople, the heart of the Byzantine Empire. Meanwhile other Muslim forces had destroyed the main Persian army and the Persian Empire fell under their control. In all the lands which they conquered, some of them the most Romanized and Christianized of the old Roman Empire, Islam eventually became the dominant religion and Arabic replaced Greek and Latin.

The motives and reasons for the spectacular success of the Muslims are subjects of continuing speculation and debate among scholars. Their armies appear to have been inspired by a mixture of religious zeal and desire for pillage. Religious enthusiasm convinced them that they were carrying out the will of God, and the ease with which they acquired wealth and plunder impelled them onward. The Arab conquerors were not engaged in a crusade to convert non-believers to Islam; they did not carry out mass conversions. Indeed they expected to remain a separate Islamic people, ruling over and collecting taxes from their subjects. Nevertheless during the course of their conquests many Christians were converted, and many non-Arabs, some of them slaves, joined their armies.

The Muslim invaders of Spain were an ethnic mixture, most of them probably Berbers from North Africa, a strain that was strengthened by later immigration. The Spanish Muslims are often called Moors, a term apparently related to Morocco, from which some of them had come. They were by no means a monolithic and united people, but were frequently at war among themselves. At first they owed allegiance to the caliph in Damascus, but in the tenth century (929) a separate caliphate was established in Spain with Córdoba as the capital city. Under the caliphate Muslim-Spanish power and culture were at their height, and Spain became the richest and most populous country in western Europe.

Muslims introduced rice, sugar, and other products not grown before in Spain and made widespread use of irrigation. Stock raising and mining were carried on successfully in Spain, as was extensive trading throughout the Mediterranean world. Such products as steel weapons, leather ware, fine textiles, and rugs were imported from the Islamic cities in the east. In turn Spanish craftsmen learned to make many of these products. An important innovation, introduced from China through Persia, was the making of paper to replace parchment. This reduced costs and facilitated production of literature and scientific studies.

Córdoba in particular was a brilliant center of Muslim culture and luxury. There one could see many elegant palaces and public buildings, as well as mosques, parks, gardens, and public baths (similar to those of ancient Rome), and the fountains found in all Muslim countries.

In the tenth and eleventh centuries Córdoba was the leading center of scholarship and literature in Europe. The intellectual and cultural achievements of the Muslims in Spain, as elsewhere, rested on the Greco-Roman culture transmitted through Byzantium and Persia. Contributions of Muslims in mathematics, chemistry, botany, optics, and medicine rested on classical scholarship. Particularly important for the later intellectual and cultural history of western Europe was Muslim Spain's transmission of much of the heritage of ancient Greece. The works of Plato and Aristotle in Arabic translation were brought to Spain along with translations of other important

Greek philosophical and scientific works. These in turn were translated into Latin and made available to western scholars.

After an initial period of conquest and plunder, Muslim rule of the subject people in Spain was relatively mild. Lands of the Visigoth state and the Christian church were confiscated, but usually not private holdings. Most of the revenue of the Moorish state came from taxes on non-Islamic people—Christians, who were known as *Mozarabs*, and Jews—but they were probably not more burdensome than taxes under the Visigoths. Christians living in rural communities were little affected by the conquest, but in the cities some restrictions were imposed. Christians were not allowed to seek new converts or build new churches, and both Christians and Jews were required to wear distinctive dress. Although the Muslims did not actively seek converts, many Christians became Muslims, perhaps a majority of those in Andalusia and Granada, where Moorish rule was more firmly established and lasted longer than elsewhere. The high percentage of Muslims was also due in part to migration of some Christians from the south to the Christian states of the north. Reasons for conversion to Islam were no doubt mixed. Many Muslim men took Christian wives who, along with their descendants, became Muslims. The nature of the Islamic religion, the simplicity of its requirements, and the contrast of Islam and Islamic society with the self-abnegation and asceticism demanded of Christians undoubtedly attracted some converts. Moreover, Muslims were free from taxes imposed on Christians.

Jews, who were numerous in some communities, were on the whole well treated. Córdoba in fact became an important center of Jewish scholarship.

Although tolerant and egalitarian in these respects, Islamic society was a male-dominated one in which women occupied an inferior position. In lands conquered by Muslim armies large numbers of women were enslaved, and traffic in women continued to be common in Muslim societies. Islamic law permitted a man to have four wives. A harem in which wives and concubines were kept in strict seclusion was a status symbol for wealthy and powerful men.

Slavery, which had existed under Roman and Visigoth rule, was widespread under Moorish rule. Slave trading flourished, especially in women. One mitigating feature was a law which provided that Christian and Jewish slaves who converted to Islam were freed.

During the latter part of the eleventh century the caliphate fragmented into a number of petty Moorish kingdoms often at war with one another. The tolerant treatment of religious minorities also ended. The advance of the Reconquest by Christian armies led some of these petty kings to appeal for help to the Muslims in North Africa. There followed in the twelfth century successive invasions by armies of two Berber groups—the Almoravids and the Almohads, the latter for a short time gaining control of all Muslim Spain. Although their armies did not stop the Christian advance, their appearance ended the era of toleration of Christians and Jews. Both groups were zealous recent converts to Islam. Their persecutions caused many Jews to migrate northward to the Christian state of Castile.

The Christian States and the Beginnings of the Reconquest

The legend and folklore about the Christian states of northern Spain and the Reconquest from the Muslims had lasting influence in shaping Spanish character and the Spaniards' view of themselves. We should not, however, paint a picture of unremitting opposition and struggle. In fact, says one modern historian, "Probably at no stage did the simple ideology of crusade really apply in the [Iberian] peninsula. Motives and relationships were always mixed" (Collins, 183). Christians fought each other as well as Muslims, and Muslims fought Muslims and were not unremitting in their efforts to destroy the Christian states. On both sides desire for plunder was often a more important motive than religion.

After the initial defeats by the Muslims, remnants of the Visigoth armies, a few nobles, and bishops took refuge in the tiny states of Asturias and Leon in the mountains in the north. Gradually a number of Christian states broke away to become independent kingdoms which were economically and culturally less advanced than Muslim Spain. There was intermittent fighting between Christians and Muslims, but at times relations were amicable. As the Christians advanced into frontier areas, in many places largely depopulated, monasteries and monastic orders played an important part in resettlement, particularly in the Duero valley. Grants of land given to the religious orders were in turn allotted to small holders. Settlements grew up around the monasteries, which served as fortresses and centers of trade. Other land grants were made to military leaders who in turn granted charters for towns and allotted lands to settlers.

The break-up of the caliphate of Córdoba and signs of growing dissension among the Muslims allowed the Christians to begin a more concerted offensive in the eleventh century. Their armies pushed southward, annexing territory or reducing Muslim states to tribute-paying status. A victory by the combined forces of several Christian states in Andalusia in 1212 was the turning point in the Christian Reconquest. The power of the Almohads was broken, they were driven back to Africa, and the small Muslim states were absorbed by the Christian kingdoms.

During the early stages of the Reconquest a number of small Christian states had emerged, each with its own distinctive character. Wars among them were frequent, but gradually they were conquered or absorbed by two powerful kingdoms, Aragon and Castile. Aragon, originally a landlocked state, expanded to include the coastal areas of Catalonia and Valencia and their important cities of Barcelona and Valencia. Castile, which became the more extensive and powerful of the two, began as a sparsely populated state in the arid plateau of north central Spain. In the north it absorbed the states of Asturias, Leon, and Galicia. In the later stages of the Reconquest Castile annexed Andalusia, with its important port of Seville. By 1276, except for the state of Granada in the extreme south, all the Muslim states had been reconquered. A Spain which was far from united, but which was Christian, had been restored.

The question of the Muslim legacy in Christian Spain has been a subject of continuing debate among scholars. Because the Reconquest involved change over a long period of time and over a wide geographical area, Muslim culture was gradually effaced or fused with Christian culture. Specifically Muslim survivals are difficult to distinguish. The degree of Muslim influence on Spanish art and architecture is debatable, but some survivals are evident in domestic architecture and furnishings and even in Christian churches and cloisters, where delicate columns and details of decorations show Arab influence. Remains of Moorish mosques have been incorporated into later buildings—notably the cathedral at Córdoba, which emerged from the great mosque, and the tower of the minaret in the cathedral at Seville. Moriscos (Muslims converted to Christianity) provided some of the labor to build Christian churches, and Muslims left a legacy of fine craftsmanship which has survived.

Some scholars see evidences of Muslim influences in later Spanish literature. All agree as to the importance to western Europe of the transmission of Greek philosophy and science via the Arabic translations brought to Spain, but the influence of these writings was probably greater in the countries north of the Pyrenees than in Spain itself.

There is general agreement that the most pervasive and lasting influence of the long struggle against the Muslims was to reinforce and strengthen the importance of Roman Catholicism in Spanish culture and among the Spanish people: "The principal effect of the Islamic confrontation with Hispanic Christian society was not by orientalization of that society, but rather the development of a distinct Hispano-Christian culture within western culture, a subculture whose attitudes and values were shaped not by Islam but by a centuries long process of warfare and confrontation" (Payne, 23).

PART II

THE SPAIN OF FERDINAND AND ISABELLA

The Catholic Monarchs

In 1469 the marriage of Isabella, who became Queen of Castile in 1474, and Ferdinand, who became King of Aragon in 1479, united the two most powerful states in Spain. "On the fragile foundation of the marriage," says one writer, "Spain's future was to be built. Inheriting distinct and mutually hostile kingdoms shattered by social and political strife, Ferdinand and Isabella [nevertheless] left to their Habsburg successors the making of a nation state ... powerful beyond any in Europe" (Lynch, 1).

The union between Ferdinand and Isabella was only a personal one. It did not merge Aragon and Castile, which continued to be ruled separately under their own governmental and legal systems. "Spain," lacking a tradition of unity and national institutions, remained a geographical term and not the name of a state. Ferdinand and Isabella were never known officially as the king and queen of Spain. But in their joint reign they took a number of steps which strengthened the monarchy and a feeling of being Spanish among their subjects.

The king of Aragon ruled over a loose confederation of states in Spain—Aragon, Catalonia, and Valencia—each of which had its own distinctive character and institutions. The power and prestige of the Aragonese kingdom was based on trade. Barcelona was the center of a commercial system which extended over the entire Mediterranean. In addition to his Spanish possessions the king of Aragon was also ruler of the islands of Sicily and Sardinia, and in 1504 Naples on the Italian mainland was added to his realm.

When Ferdinand took the throne, Aragon was declining in strength, partly as the result of loss of population from the Black Death, which had ravaged the coastal areas in the fourteenth century. As commerce shifted from the Mediterranean to the Atlantic during the next century the decline in her fortunes continued.

Castile, on the other hand, more centrally located and possessing far more territory and population than Aragon, was a dynamic state. As we have seen, it had expanded over much of the peninsula, gaining access to the Atlantic in the northwest and also in the southwest, where it had acquired the great commercial city of Seville. Although Andalusia had suffered serious depopulation from the Black Death, the central and northern parts of the kingdom of Castile were less affected. The monarch of Castile had gained extensive power and could act independently while the ruler of Aragon was more restricted by regional assemblies (*cortes*).

Castile was clearly destined to become the dominant partner. In their marriage contract Isabella placed limits on Ferdinand's authority over her realm. Isabella became a real queen with a mind of her own. She was deeply religious but her piety did not prevent her being ruthless and opportunistic. Some decisions and policies were clearly hers, but for the most part she and Ferdinand worked together harmoniously and shared common goals.

Theirs was not a love match, but Isabella had insisted in the face of opposition on marrying Ferdinand in preference to others, perhaps because she saw in the union a means of gaining personal power and creating a powerful and united Spain. Ferdinand, for his part, brought shrewdness and diplomatic ability to the match. He was scheming and unscrupulous, reputed to have been a model for Machiavelli's Prince. He was quite willing to concede the dominant position of Castile, but after she became queen Isabella gave her husband full power to act without her in Castile. After her death in 1516 Ferdinand served as regent in Castile.

The Spain of Ferdinand and Isabella

The rule of Ferdinand and Isabella, who chose to be known as "The Catholic Monarchs" (*Los Reyes Catolicos*), was of a very personal nature. They did not delegate authority for making important decisions. They were the only rulers in the history of Spain to visit all the cities and large towns in their realm and to live in each for several weeks at a time. This practice drained resources since the monarchs were accompanied by large retinues, but it helped to develop a personal loyalty to the rulers. There was no single capital of Castile as yet; the capital was the place where the monarchs resided at any given time.

A principal goal of the Catholic Monarchs was to enhance royal power and authority, but in order to achieve this they followed a pattern of compromise and concession with powerful and privileged groups—reducing some of their power but at the same time guaranteeing that they retain some of their privileges. To strengthen their own power they needed to reduce the powers of three groups—a powerful aristocracy, the clergy, and the governments of towns and cities which had been largely self-governing during the Middle Ages.

An extremely powerful aristocracy had been created over the centuries by earlier rulers who had given away land and power in order to win military support. Great lords ruled almost like kings over vast tracts of land, and controlled private armies, administration of justice, and immense wealth from income from their lands. During the first years of their reign the Catholic Monarchs faced a number of uprisings against their authority, but one of their important achievements as rulers was the pacification of the great lords and the limitation of their political power. Ferdinand and Isabella preferred to use conciliatory methods, but when necessary they used military force, razing castles and confiscating land. Private armies were abolished, the political power of the nobles broken, but they retained a privileged position before the law and freedom from royal taxation. Moreover Ferdinand and Isabella rewarded loyal followers and successful military commanders by granting new titles of nobility.

Creation of a national Castilian militia directly under royal command was also important in curbing the nobles and other dissident groups. Used at first to achieve internal peace, it became the nucleus for the Spanish army which was to fight in foreign wars. Administration of justice was another area where the Catholic Monarchs tried to strengthen royal authority and bring about greater uniformity. There were many conflicting jurisdictions and different systems of law throughout Spain. Ferdinand and Isabella reduced the power of the great nobles and increased the jurisdiction of royal courts of justice. They themselves frequently exercised their royal prerogatives by intervening personally in various cases, and they constituted the court of last appeal. The monarchs interfered more than their predecessors in the internal affairs of the cities, which had earlier been largely independent. They built up the power of an urban elite loyal to them by changes in methods of selecting members of the municipal councils. At the same time their interference stopped factional fighting and brought greater order and stability.

Since medieval times *cortes*, political assemblies consisting of representatives of the nobility, clergy, and towns, had existed in every Spanish kingdom. In Castile, where they were less powerful than in Aragon, they had no inherent powers. Laws were made by royal authority, the *cortes* having only the power to petition and advise. One function of the *cortes* was to vote a financial subsidy (*servicio*) at the request of the monarch — usually to finance a war. Ferdinand and Isabella were less dependent on the *cortes* for financial support than earlier rulers because they developed other sources of revenue, but they continued to call meetings of the assemblies. They usually made laws in the presence of the *cortes* of Castile although they were not required to do so.

The monarchs issued numerous edicts and regulations affecting the economy but they had no coherent economic policies. While centralizing political control under the monarchy, they did not take steps to create an economic unit—to integrate all regions of Spain. Their policies were intended to benefit

Castile rather than the whole of Spain and to gain revenue for the royal treasury. Barriers to trade between Aragon and Castile continued to the detriment of the former. Two economies continued, one oriented toward the Mediterranean, the other to the growing importance of the Atlantic. As we shall see, settlement and exploitation of the Spanish possessions in the New World and commerce between them and Spain became largely a Castilian monopoly.

The Catholic Monarchs showed no interest in improving the condition of the peasants and laborers who made up the vast majority of the population. In favoring certain privileged groups—the great landowners of Castile and Castilian wool merchants—they have been criticized by modern historians for inhibiting the development of a balanced economy and making Spain dependent on other countries for necessary food and manufactured goods. One writer has described agriculture as the "Cinderella of the Castilian economy" (Elliott, *Imperial Spain*, 117). The prime example was the privileged position of sheep growers, who were great nobles, and wool merchants. The monarchs protected and guaranteed the special privileges of the *Mesta*, the organization of the owners of vast sheep raising estates in Castile and Andalusia. The favored treatment was due in part to the fact that wool was the principal export of Castile and taxes on it an important source of revenue. Small farmers suffered as the result of the land monopoly of the sheep growers. Because sheep herding required fewer persons than growing cereal crops, farm tenants were put off the land. As a consequence, probably unforeseen, those displaced tenants furnished manpower for the armies that conquered Granada, fought in Europe, and conquered and settled Spain's possessions in the New World. As a result of the favored treatment of wool the cities along the northern coast of Spain developed a flourishing trade with the cities of the Netherlands and other parts of northern Europe.

One of the most significant achievements of the Catholic Monarchs was the control they gained over the Church, the most powerful institution in Spain. In doing this they enhanced royal authority and at the same time gained independence from papal control. It is a paradox of Spanish history that Spain, the most Catholic of countries, was also the most free from control by the Pope in Rome.

The Spanish church was an immensely wealthy, powerful, and privileged institution, and the monarchs did not openly challenge it. Instead they summoned an ecclesiastical council at Seville and won the support of the Spanish bishops for certain reforms, the most important of which gave the monarchs control over all major ecclesiastical appointments. A papal bull of 1486 gave them ecclesiastical patronage (*patronato*) over all church appointments to be made as the result of the reconquest of the Muslim kingdom of Granada. This was important not only because of the power it gave the crown in Granada, but also because it served as a precedent for royal authority in the expansion of Christianity into the New World. In the twenty years following the voyage of Columbus in 1492 the Spanish monarchy won control over ecclesiastical appointments, missionary activity, and collection of church tithes in the newly discovered lands. This was the foundation of the extraordinary control of the state over the Church in Hispanic America. By the end of the reign of the Catholic Monarchs the crown had gained power over most appointments and conferring of benefices—i.e. control over property and income which went with the appointment—in Spain itself.

Another religious policy regarded by Ferdinand and Isabella as a reform and at the same time a means of strengthening the state was the Inquisition, which will be dealt with at greater length at a later time. But it is appropriate to notice it here as a part of the overall program of the Catholic Monarchs. The Inquisition, a special court set up to investigate and punish heresy, was not a Spanish invention. An Inquisition directly responsible to the Pope had been established in the thirteenth century to deal with the Albigensian heresy, which centered in France. The distinctive feature of the Inquisition under Ferdinand and Isabella was that it was a *Spanish* Inquisition, under the authority of the Spanish monarchs. The tribunal, which began operations in 1483, was under the direct control of the crown, at first in Castile but later in Aragon as well. It was

The Spain of Ferdinand and Isabella

the only governmental institution which was common to all of Spain. The motivation for its establishment appears to have been primarily religious, but it had an importance beyond religion, serving as a symbol of monarchy as well as Church and fostering a spirit of national identity among all Spaniards as true Christians.

In the conquest of Granada, the final step in the Reconquest, a mixture of motives—religious, political, and economic—also played a part. A holy war against the last Muslim state in Spain (one which already paid tribute to Castile) would strengthen Christianity, help to unite Spain, and enrich the conquerors. A crusading spirit had already been aroused by the Pope's calls for resistance to the Ottoman Turks, a Muslim people who had conquered Constantinople in 1453 and were expanding their power over the Mediterranean. The war against Granada, begun in 1482, went on for ten years. Fighting in mountainous terrain, the Spanish infantry gained experience which would later make them successful in European campaigns outside of Spain. After all the other strongholds in the kingdom had been taken, the city of Granada agreed to negotiate and surrendered to Ferdinand on January 2, 1492.

The terms of the surrender were remarkably generous. The new Muslim subjects of Castile were to be governed by their own local magistrates under their own system of law. They were to pay no more taxes than under the earlier regime. More important, they were guaranteed the right to practice their own religion. The promise of liberal treatment and toleration was due in part to hopes of placating this large minority and ultimately winning them to Christianity. The monarchy, not yet firmly established, apparently hoped by generous treatment to prevent the Granadians from conspiring with the Muslim peoples of North Africa.

The hoped for harmonious relations between conquerors and conquered did not develop. Almost immediately the crown began a program of forcible conversions to Christianity, which led to rebellion and bitter resentment among the Moriscos, a problem bequeathed by the Catholic Monarchs to their successors.

Immediately after the surrender of Granada, also in 1492, another drastic step to achieve religious unity was taken after long deliberation. On March 30 the Catholic Monarchs signed an edict ordering the expulsion of all professed Jews (not the *conversos*, the converts to Christianity) within four months. Anti-Semitism had been strengthened by the Inquisition, some cities having ordered expulsion earlier. Expulsion of Jews, it was argued, would remove the temptation of *conversos* to revert to Judaism. Some Jews hastily converted to Christianity to avoid expulsion, thus adding to the number of *conversos* and fueling popular suspicion of the orthodoxy of *conversos*. On the other hand some *conversos*, fearful of the future in Spain, joined their fellow Jews in exile.

In addition to the conquest of Granada and the expulsion of the Jews a third epoch-making event took place in 1492. On April 17 Christopher Columbus received a commission and promise of support from the Catholic Monarchs for his historic voyage, remembered in America and elsewhere as the most important event of the reign of Ferdinand and Isabella. Under them conquest and expansion into the New World began, and colonial policies began to take shape—subjects we will deal with later. Ferdinand and Isabella could not, of course, foresee the consequences of these beginnings. They themselves evidently considered the completion of the Reconquest their most important achievement and chose to be buried in the Cathedral at Granada.

The union of the crowns of Aragon and Castile and the reign of the Catholic Monarchs were important steps toward the emergence of a Spanish nation, but the process was far from complete. Columbus, for example, discovered the New World in the name of Castile, not Spain. Still, the monarchs had brought about a large degree of peace and internal stability. They had enhanced the power of the monarchy and reduced the political powers of the great nobles, but not their economic power and privileges. They had succeeded in weakening the prerogatives of

Rome and controlled a church which was closely identified with the monarchy and the state. But the Church remained a powerful and privileged institution. The attempt at achieving religious unity and a Christian Spain untainted by heterodoxy had not been completely successful and came at a tremendous cost to the social fabric of Spain. There had been protests from some quarters over the methods of the Inquisition, and some cities had protested over the economic consequences of the expulsion of the Jews, but Ferdinand and Isabella prized religious unity over other considerations.

Society and Social Classes

A sixteenth century writer describes contemporary Spain as follows:

> The mountains which cross Spain on every side are neither cultivated nor embellished with villages as in France. They consist of huge, bare, and jagged rocks which are called *sierras* or *peñas*. If they are smaller and covered with trees, the people call them *monts* and pasture their cattle on them. Between them are plains of very even ground, like those in Castile; for the most part they are not cultivated except around the big towns and for a league and a half around the villages. The villages are so far apart that one can sometimes ride a whole day without seeing a living soul, except perhaps an occasional shepherd tending his flocks.
>
> (Defourneaux, 17)

Disasters in the fourteenth century—crop failures which caused starvation, followed by the Black Death (bubonic plague)—drastically reduced population over large areas, some of them remaining nearly depopulated for generations. During the fifteenth century numbers were further reduced by civil wars. At the beginning of the sixteenth century the population of Spain was estimated at about seven million, while France, a country of comparable size, had a population more than twice as great. Nevertheless nearly all of the people in Spain lived in communities—villages, towns, or cities. The majority, small farmers or agricultural workers, lived in tiny unincorporated villages. Each day they left the village to work in the fields, returning home at night.

The remainder lived in incorporated towns and cities. A strong urban tradition dated back to the centuries of Roman rule. During the Reconquest, as the frontier was pushed south, charters (*fueros*) were granted to municipalities in order to attract settlers to depopulated areas. Those charters defined the local government and the rights of its citizens. The incorporated area included not only the center where people lived but also a perimeter of farm land. The terms of the *fueros* varied but all gave the corporations a large amount of control over their affairs. As in so many other things, this pattern was continued in the New World—one of Cortés' first actions was to found such a municipality, Vera Cruz.

Towns and cities were centers of religious, economic, social, and cultural life. Nobles might have castles in the countryside but they chose to live in palaces in the cities. Cities varied in size and character. Seville, the great commercial center, was the most cosmopolitan and probably the richest. Madrid, hitherto of no particular importance, grew in size and wealth after Philip II designated it as the capital of his Spanish realm. There were forty bishoprics in Spain, each of them containing a cathedral, usually the most impressive building in the city. There were many other churches, monasteries, and convents in the towns and cities, evidence of the wealth and power of the Church. Palaces and houses of the nobles and the urban elite dominated some quarters. In other sections were the houses of the poor, often little more than hovels. Every town had its local market, and in the large cities were markets and fairs, center of trade for large areas, thronged with merchants from Spain and other countries.

For the working classes life was hard, poverty the normal condition. But there were many Holy Days and diversions to break the monotony. Holy Days of religious significance were also days for spectacular processions and festivals where people of all social classes mingled. The Spanish had a great love of the theater, which, as we shall see, was religious in origin. The golden age of drama, of Lope de Vega and Calderon de la Barca, began late in the sixteenth century, but numerous playwrights preceded them. Only in the large cities were there buildings constructed for theatrical performances, but groups of traveling players visited even small towns, presenting their performances in open squares on makeshift stages. Puppet shows and circuses also furnished entertainment.

Spaniards of all classes danced—dancing was a national pastime. At the royal court and in aristocratic society dances were formal and ceremonial, to stately musical accompaniment. Among the lower classes dancing to the accompaniment of guitars and tamborines was livelier, sometimes almost frenzied.

There were various kinds of tournaments and competitions. Some towns commemorated past victories over Moors by mock battles, fought in elaborate costumes. Bullfights were forerunners of today's national pastime, occasions of tradition and elaborate ceremony. Enthusiasm for these spectacles was shared by all social classes, but the participants were members of the aristocracy for whom these contests furnished opportunity to demonstrate skill and bravery.

In spite of the growing authority of the monarchy a powerful and privileged aristocracy continued to dominate society, attitudes, and values, and much of the wealth of Spain. Less than half of the land in Spain was subject to the direct authority of the crown. The remainder consisted of *tierra de señorío*, great estates subject to the direct authority of a *señor*, or lord. This privileged group, comprising a tiny fraction of the entire population, acquired their wealth and power through a variety of means over a long period of time. The seigniorial system had originated in the twelfth century as a royal delegation of jurisdiction to an individual at a time when kings needed to build up strong allies in reconquering and repopulating territory won from Muslim control. Over the centuries some nobles had acquired holdings which were almost small kingdoms, independent of royal control in practice if not in theory. For example, the Mendoza family, which had estates scattered over Spain, controlled 258 towns and villages and appointed more than 500 public officers.

Ferdinand and Isabella opposed granting away royal land and jurisdiction. But under their successors, Charles V and

Philip II, more large holdings of royal land were sold to nobles who wanted to increase their holdings, and to wealthy merchants eager to attain noble status. The sales were one way of increasing revenue to meet expenses and to pay interest on the staggering national debt, but in making them the kings diminished the power of the crown. Under traditional Spanish law all heirs shared in the inheritance when a father died. This practice, which had the effect of dividing land holdings, was modified by a law of 1505 which established the right of *mayorazgos*, similar to entail, which made land inalienable and prevented it from being divided. The *mayorazgo*, too, was adopted in the New World, where Cortés owned one of the largest Spanish estates.

The various ranks of aristocrats were formalized by Charles V. At the very top were the titled nobles (dukes, counts, etc.), of whom there were twenty-five grandees who possessed certain honorific privileges—wearing their hats in the presence of the monarch and addressing him as "cousin." Below them were thirty-five titled but less privileged nobles. The remainder were untitled *caballeros* and *hidalgos*, gentry of modest means who were, however, entitled to use the prefix of *"Don."*

There was some social mobility in the system, several ways of acquiring noble status. Sometimes it was given as a grant for military service, sometimes for holding high public office, and sometimes by purchase. Wealth from mines and investments in the New World might be used to buy noble status in Spain. But however the rank was achieved, one outward sign was the right to display a family coat of arms. There were also certain legal privileges. In criminal cases persons of noble rank could not be tortured or sentenced to the galleys. Nor could they be imprisoned for debt. Most important, they were exempt from paying royal taxes.

The vast majority of the population, of course, were neither nobility nor clergy. The only distinction they had in common was the lack of the privileges of the other two orders. Most of them were peasants—small farmers and agricultural laborers. In

The Spain of Ferdinand and Isabella

the cities most were common laborers, but some were artisans, businessmen, merchants, and professionals.

Although peasants made up most of the population they were rarely mentioned by contemporary writers, and records about them are sparse. They themselves were largely illiterate, and illiterates leave few records for posterity. There were many regional and local differences in systems of land-holding and differences in the economic condition of the peasants. As we have seen, vast areas were under the system of *señorios*, subject to allotment by the lord; the remainder were royal lands. Some farmers held land under leaseholds or contractual agreements; others owned their land. On lands allotted by the lords, taxes and rents went to the lord; on royal lands, most of which were in Castile, taxes and dues went to the crown.

Wheat and barley were the principal crops on peasant lands. The cultivated fields were in a perimeter around the town or village—near enough that it was possible for workers to go back and forth to the fields daily. Yields of crops were generally mediocre because of the arid climate and primitive tools. As in most of Europe, much of the land lay fallow every other year, or sometimes two out of three years, to restore fertility. In some places irrigation ditches, filled with water from nearby streams fed by melting snow from the mountains, helped to make up for lack of rainfall in spring and summer, but irrigation was limited. To build dams which would conserve the water from the torrential rains of autumn and winter was beyond the engineering ability of the times.

Outside the area of cultivated fields was empty land (*baldios*), used by the villagers and townspeople for grazing sheep and goats and gathering firewood. But peasant communities in the sixteenth century were increasingly faced with the loss of these common lands by encroachments from the great landholders, who began to bring them under cultivation. Peasants also complained that flocks belonging to members of the powerful *Mesta* sometimes grazed on the common land and fallow fields.

Patterns of agriculture varied from region to region. In the fertile valley of the Ebro River and in Valencia orange groves and olive orchards flourished. In Andalusia, where grapes and olives were important, some of the vast estates were worked by laborers from the towns who found seasonal employment in the orchards and vineyards.

There appears to be general agreement among scholars that the number of peasants who had held land as freeholds in earlier centuries was declining as more and more land was incorporated into large estates. A survey by Philip II showed that peasants owned the land they worked only in exceptional cases. The survey gave abundant evidence of the growing poverty and oppression of the peasants toward the end of the sixteenth century—a subject to be dealt with in greater detail below. Even the *cortes* of Castile commented in 1598 that "everything tends toward the destruction of the poor peasantry and the increase in property, authority and power of the rich" (quoted in Kamen, 111). Peasants bore the burden of taxation but received none of the benefits. Their money went to support the luxury of the royal establishment, a host of office holders, and, most important, the cost of the military.

The lowest rung of the social order was occupied by a class not yet mentioned—slaves. Slavery had existed in Spain since ancient times. During the Moorish conquest and occupation many Christians had been enslaved; later during the period of the Reconquest Christians enslaved Muslims. On both sides the right to enslave infidels and heathen was generally regarded as legitimate. By the fifteenth century most slaves in Spain were Muslims captured in the Reconquest or their descendants. The supply was substantially increased by the campaign against Granada and numbers continued to grow as the result of Spanish military campaigns in North Africa. In these same campaigns Muslims continued to capture Christians and enslave them. Some black African slaves transported overland from the sub-Sahara by caravans had been brought to Spain long before the opening of the Atlantic slave trade, their numbers increasing as the result of that trade in which the Portuguese took the lead.

They were most numerous in Andalusia and particularly in Seville, where they made up a sizeable part of the population.

Most slaves, male and female, were used for domestic service, performing a variety of tasks. In wealthy households ownership of slaves, especially blacks who served as personal attendants, was a status symbol. Some were also purchased as capital investments to work as artisans or to be hired out by their owners.

One theory held that conversion to Christianity freed one from bondage, but in practice this did not occur. In fact the Church showed concern for slaves who were Christians, and masters often took pains with religious instruction. Masters also frequently emancipated their slaves by will or during the owner's lifetime.

Although evidence is sketchy, treatment of slaves seems to have been relatively mild. Slavery in the Iberian Peninsula bore little resemblance to the plantation slavery developed in the Spanish and Portuguese colonies in the New World, but precedents for the labor system developed in America were found in sugar growing in the Canary Islands and the islands of the Mediterranean.

Strikingly absent in Spanish society was any substantial group that might be classified as a "middle class" in either the economic or social sense. Only a small number—perhaps as few as four percent in 1500—would not have been classed as aristocrats or peasant-laborers. Their numbers grew during the sixteenth century but still remained a small fraction of the whole. They included successful farmers, merchants, owners of small industries, and professional men—lawyers, medical doctors, and notaries, many of whom were Jews or *conversos*. The decision of Ferdinand and Isabella to expel the Jews and the fear of the Inquisition which caused *conversos* to leave weakened the prospects for the development of a middle class.

The virtual absence of a bourgeoisie, which was to have important consequences for the future of Spain, was due in part to social values and attitudes. A pro-aristocratic mentality, a prejudice against business and commerce, existed among all classes. Successful merchants were likely to use their profits to buy land and acquire aristocratic status. There were many examples of this, particularly in Seville, which had a monopoly on the American trade. Wealth from trade and investments in the New World went to buy land and acquire aristocratic status in Spain. On the other hand, the dazzling prospects of riches from the New World led some landed aristocrats of Seville to invest in trade. "Two parallel currents ... operated in Seville.... One was the commercialization of the nobility and the other the ennoblement of the merchants" (Pike, 99). Many of those merchants, however, were foreigners, Genoese in particular, men "not paralyzed by aristocratic prejudices," who were drawn to Spain by the prospect of wealth through trade.

Prejudice against business was related to disdain for all forms of labor. "In a society where standards were set by the landed aristocracy there were few prospects for labourers and artisans. The Spanish working class of the sixteenth century, confronted by a prosperous nobility whose estate was a magnet for manufacturers and merchants, had visible evidence for the view that work was degrading" (Lynch, 116). In the absence of a middle class which they might have hoped to enter, peasants and artisans could not regard work as a means for improving their status. Members of these classes worked because the only alternative was starvation, but there was no concept of the dignity of labor or hard work as a means of upward mobility.

Obsession with aristocratic status was closely related to the Spanish obsession with *honor*. One writer says that there were two elements in the soul of Spain, "The Catholic faith and concern for one's honour" (Defourneaux, 36). This concept of honor, which had little to do with morality but involved a code of conduct, set aristocrats from the poorest *hidalgos* to the greatest nobles apart from the rest of society. Heredity was an important element, with increasing emphasis on "purity of blood" (*limpieza de sangre*). The importance of untainted ancestry was intensified by the Inquisition and the expulsion of Jews, but it had existed earlier. Conversion to Christianity did not entirely remove the stigma of Jewish or Moorish ancestry. Purity of blood laws, which imposed disabilities on *conversos*, were widely adopted. An early and extreme example was the Toledo law of 1449 which declared that *conversos*, "offspring of perverse and Jewish ancestors," were unworthy to hold public office or ecclesiastical appointments or to exercise any sort of authority over "the true Christians of the Holy Catholic Church" (Defourneaux, 26).

In Spain, as in most societies, what we know of women is gleaned almost entirely from the writings of men, evidence that is likely to be biased and fragmentary. Much of Spanish literature of the Golden Age—novels, dramas, poetry—was concerned with women, but the women of literature were likely to be exceptional rather than typical. In literature peasant women, the vast majority of the sex, are rarely mentioned.

In Spain, as in the other Christian countries of western Europe, which inherited vestiges of Roman law, women had legal rights denied them in most societies. One institution which distinguished Christian from Muslim Spain was monogamous marriage. Spanish law provided that all children of a marriage, daughters as well as sons, shared in the inheritance of the parents' estate. Under Visigothic law, which was adapted from the Roman, women inherited real estate as well as moveable property. Women were parties to contracts and their consent was necessary to the sale of property. Primogeniture (inheritance of the estate by the eldest son), which was a part of English Common Law, did not exist in Spain, but the laws of some communities permitted a limited degree of preferential treatment, and the system of *mayorazgos* mentioned above allowed part of an estate to be made inalienable and assigned to the eldest son. Sometimes daughters inherited land; sometimes their dowry was their part of a father's estate. After marriage a woman continued to control her share of an estate. Property of a married couple was held in common and could not be sold without the consent of both. However, in spite of property rights, women by no means enjoyed complete legal equality with men. For example, adultery by a wife was punishable as a crime, but not adultery by a husband.

Although women inherited estates and had property rights they had no part in public affairs. Spain was indeed a very masculine society. Spanish literature and the accounts of travelers suggest that women of the upper classes led secluded and idle lives of luxury. Perhaps as a legacy of Muslim culture, custom dictated that these women were largely confined to their homes. The honor of husbands required that the reputation of their wives be above reproach, hence the necessity for sheltering and protecting them.

Before marriage young girls were kept under strict supervision and were carefully chaperoned. They had few contacts with boys and men, except for their fathers and brothers. Yet we know that some girls dreamed of romantic love, sometimes escaping from parental vigilance and engaging in furtive flirtations. However, marriages were arranged by parents. Daughters who married without family consent could be disinherited. Once espoused, a girl could go to various outings and social events with her fiance, but always accompanied by a chaperon.

Women of the upper classes lived in large houses, luxuriously furnished and richly decorated, spending their days at home, supervising the care of children, embroidering or doing fine needlework, sometimes enjoying the company of women visitors. They were not entirely without education, though they had little or no formal schooling. Education for women was often regarded as dangerous, likely to encourage unconventional behavior. Nevertheless, some of them read widely and were even acquainted with philosophy, although most read little but works on religion and novels of romance.

While women lived secluded lives men spent most of their time away from home. Wives usually left home only to attend mass or other church-related functions, and when they did, heavily veiled and wearing capes or cloaks which enveloped them, they were accompanied by attendants. Sometimes they went in the company of their husbands to balls and public festivals. Spanish drama frequently portrayed unfaithful wives who deceived their husbands. Such women were certainly not typical of the Spanish aristocracy, but given the restricted lives they led it is not surprising that some wives sought relief from the boredom by unconventional behavior.

The lives of the great majority of women, wives of farmers, artisans, and day laborers, were very different from those of their wealthy sisters. They lived lives of hard work, keeping house, bearing and taking care of numerous children, working in the fields. But they are an anonymous group almost completely absent from literature.

Marriage and family were the center of life for nearly all women, but of necessity women of the lower classes were less sheltered and restricted than those of the aristocracy. A few owned their own small businesses, a few were employed as housekeepers, more as domestic servants, but few occupations outside the home were open to them.

Limited as is the evidence about most women of the lower classes, more information survives about the few who turned to or were forced into prostitution, a means of livelihood regulated by law in the larger cities. In every city they lived in certain sections which were supervised by "fathers" appointed by the city who were responsible for the orderly operation of the brothels. Regulations intended to protect women prohibited married women and virgins from employment and fixed the fees which clients paid. Prostitutes were not entirely ignored by the Church. During Lent they were exhorted to repent, and there were convents especially for those who repented.

At the opposite end of the spectrum from the brothel was the Church, which offered a way of life for many unmarried women. In Spain a larger percentage of both sexes belonged to religious orders than in any other country of western Europe. Women from every level of society entered convents, some of which, in fact, received only persons of noble birth. Widows of aristocratic status frequently entered convents as places of security after the deaths of their husbands, but most members came as young unmarried women. Sometimes daughters joined religious orders out of personal conviction; sometimes they were placed there involuntarily by their parents. During the reign of

Philip II one observer wrote that even the wealthiest aristocrats found it difficult to raise money for the dowries that were required if a daughter was to make a good marriage. For some the life of a nun was the only alternative to marriage. Convents for women of this class were richly endowed, the members enjoying many of the comforts and luxuries of secular society.

On the other hand, life in some orders called for dedication and austerity. For many women service to religion offered opportunities for self-fulfillment and meaningful work denied them in other vocations. Women enjoyed a wide role in religion and religious orders if they were not suspected of heresy. By far the most important and influential example was St. Teresa of Ávila, one of the greatest figures in the history of the Roman Catholic Church and one of the greatest in Spanish literature.

Born into an aristocratic family, Teresa early chose a life of religious dedication, entering the order of the Carmelites. Her great service to the Church, for which she was canonized soon after her death, was the reform and reorganization of that order. In the reform and resurgence of Catholicism, usually called the Counter Reformation (to be discussed later), her work was probably as important as that of Ignatius Loyola, who founded the Jesuit order.

In her religious experience Teresa was a mystic, sharing some of the beliefs of the mystics who were brought before the Inquisition, but she was able to remain within the Church and was not charged with heresy. Although a mystic she possessed earthy common sense, tact, and business ability as well. When she talked of organizing a new, reformed order (the so-called Discalced Carmelites), she was mocked by male members of the clergy, but she overcame obstacles, gained the respect and support of Philip II and the support of Pope Gregory III. Convents of the new order sprang up all over Spain.

As a woman Teresa had special concern for members of her sex and their role in religion. One of the obstacles that she and other women faced was disparagement by the male clergy, who held women in low esteem because of their interpretation of the Biblical story of Eve and because of the New Testament admonitions of St. Paul concerning women. While acknowledging their weakness and vulnerability, Teresa sought to reassure women and convince them that they were worthy and able to serve God, that, in fact, they possessed qualities that made them superior to men in some respects.

In addition to her work of organization and administration she wrote a number of books, one an autobiography, another a guide for the nuns of her order. The greatest of her writings is the *Castillo Interior* ("inner castle"), one of the finest works on mystical experience ever written.

Religion and the Church

"The history and culture of no other people in the world are more totally identified with Roman Catholicism than those of the people of Spain" (Payne, 3). While the Catholic Monarchs had reduced the power of Rome over the Church in Spain and gained for themselves the right to make most appointments and to control finances, the Church remained wealthy and powerful and the clergy a privileged class.

The clergy consisted of two groups—regular (members of religious orders) and secular, ranging from parish priests to bishops. Persons of all classes and social backgrounds joined the clergy, from peasants and artisans to aristocrats, but members of the lower classes seldom rose in the church hierarchy. The higher clergy were often members of the highest ranks of the aristocracy and persons of great wealth. Some were men of high moral purpose; others were as worldly as their counterparts in secular society. Owing their appointments to the crown, they were strong supporters of the monarchy. Many high administrators of the state were drawn from the clergy, particularly under Philip II. Although they were exempt from taxes, as were the lay aristocracy, they often made large contributions to the state, sometimes under royal pressure. For example, the Bishop of Toledo, whose see was the richest in Christendom outside of Rome, gave Philip a large grant for his war against England, which was regarded by Catholics as a religious war.

A higher percentage of the population entered the ranks of the clergy in Spain than in any other country in western Europe, probably because opportunities for other kinds of employment and for social advancement were limited. A bishop, writing in 1624, admitted: "There are some who say that religion now has become a way of earning a living and that many take to religion as they would to any other trade" (quoted in Defourneaux, 108). Monasteries and convents, some with only a few members, numbered in the thousands. Some of the religious orders were entirely Spanish, founded in the period of the Reconquest; others, including the Dominicans, Carmelites, and, later, the Jesuits, were found throughout Europe.

The religious orders and bishoprics owned immense amounts of land and other forms of wealth. The crown granted them large grants of land during the Reconquest, and to the heritage of earlier centuries were added bequests and purchase of land by the religious orders. Visible evidence of the wealth of the church was everywhere, but that of Toledo was most dazzling. A visitor wrote: "It quite certainly contains more monasteries, monks and nuns than any other part of Spain and probably throughout all Christendom. The churches and monasteries alone seem to comprise the whole town.... The cathedral is not only majestic and beautiful but its treasures, even disregarding the golden reliquaries, the precious stones, and the jewels, are in my opinion unique in the world" (Defourneaux, 108).

Although for some, men more often than women, religion was perfunctory, most Spaniards adhered strictly to requirements of the Church—attendance at mass (often daily), observing days of abstinence, giving alms to the poor, veneration of the saints, and religious pilgrimages. Most famous of the shrines in Spain was Santiago de Compostela in Galicia, believed to be the burial site of Santiago (St. James, brother of Jesus), patron saint of Spanish Christians and their spiritual leader in the Reconquest.

Religion was an inward experience, but symbols and outward manifestations heightened the experience. Although there were some grim aspects (warnings of future punishments for those who strayed), many religious activities and symbols brightened the drabness and relieved the monotony of the lives of the lower classes. The magnificence of the churches, the richness of their treasures, the rituals, the music, and the incense filled participants with awe and reverence. The most impressive religious observances, processions and ceremonies, were associated with Holy Week and Corpus Christi Day. Other saint's days were observed throughout Spain, and most towns had their local saints and shrines. Religious spectacles and fetes occurred all year long. Festivities not directly connected with religion also took place on saint's days—festivals and fairs at which people from all classes mingled.

Today the development associated with religion in Spain in the minds of most people is probably the Spanish Inquisition, which was both a manifestation of religious zeal and an effort to strengthen cultural and national unity. Though Spain was not unique in its efforts to stamp out heresy and attain religious conformity, her efforts were more pervasive and of more lasting significance than those in any other country.

The religious intolerance displayed in the Inquisition and the expulsion of the Jews and Moriscos was a relatively late development. The Christian states of medieval Spain had been more tolerant of non-Christians than had been most of Europe. During the long period of the Reconquest, except for occasional outbursts of fanaticism, Christians, Muslims, and Jews had lived together peaceably. One early king of Castile, Ferdinand III, had referred to himself as "king of three religions." During the later stages of Muslim domination in the south large numbers of Jews had moved northward to escape from the persecutions of the Almohads and Almoravids, establishing communities in all the larger towns. Confined to living in designated areas (ghettos), Jews had not acquired land nor engaged in farming, but had become artisans, merchants, members of the professions, and bankers. During the late fourteenth century, a period of despair and economic disruption caused by the Black Death, there were outbursts of anti-semitism. In 1391 massacres occurred in most of the major cities. Thousands of Jews were forced to flee or accept baptism as Christians. These "new Christians" were known as *conversos*. Many of them prospered and rose to high positions in society and government and even in the Church. But their condition was an uneasy one. The genuineness of their conversion was always suspect. Although some of them were thoroughly Christian in culture as well as religion, others, while embracing the Christian faith, retained links with Jewish culture and were suspected of reverting to Jewish religious practices.

In 1478, on the advice of high clergymen, Ferdinand and Isabella applied to the Pope for permission to set up a tribunal of Inquisition in Castile, an authority which was later extended to Aragon as well. The tribunal was the only institution, and the Inquisitor General the only official, whose authority extended to the whole of Spain. The Holy Office, as it was known, was a court of justice, operating under the authority of the crown. Its purpose was to ferret out and punish heresy of professed Christians who were guilty of straying from orthodoxy. It was not concerned with professing Jews and Muslims. Because nearly all the persons brought before it were *conversos* of Jewish ancestry its operation gave an impetus to purity of blood laws and practices. Unlike other courts in Spain it made no distinction between members of different social groups. Nobles as well as laborers came under its jurisdiction.

It is important to point out that by the standards of the era in which it operated the Spanish Inquisition was not particularly cruel or unjust, nor the penalties it imposed extreme, although some contemporaries were critical of its methods and penalties. While the accused enjoyed certain guarantees including the right to legal counsel, by today's standards there were gross violations of due process. Torture was used at times to extract confessions but no more than in other courts of the period. Agents of the Inquisition traveled about collecting evidence of heresy. A suspect who confessed voluntarily was usually given a free pardon, but only on condition that he or she name others who were accomplices in heretical crimes. A person convicted might receive a lighter penalty for revealing the names of others. The secrecy of its operations was perhaps the most terrifying aspect of the Inquisition. Suspects might be arrested and carried away

The Spain of Ferdinand and Isabella

to secret prisons, where they might languish cut off from all outside communication for years, until a trial brought either acquittal or appearance before the public in an *auto de fe*.

The *auto de fe* (literally, "act of faith") was an awesome spectacle, a kind of representation of the Last Day of Judgment, designed to strike terror of the consequences of heresy in the hearts of the beholders. Before the assembled crowd the guilty were called into view and their sentences pronounced. Penalties ranged from penances of varying degrees of severity, to imprisonment, public scourging, forced labor on galleys, or death. Persons sentenced to be executed were handed over to secular authorities; the *auto de fe* was not the scene of the execution.

The stigma of guilt lingered on after the accused who were not executed had paid their penalty. Persons who had been convicted were required to wear distinctive garments which made them targets for public abuse. Their descendants also suffered from the disgrace. Purity of blood meant not only absence of Jewish or Moorish ancestry, but also evidence that no ancestor had been found guilty by the Holy Office.

The Spanish Inquisition was an enduring institution, lasting for almost three hundred and fifty years. During the first and most important phase, which lasted until about 1525, most of the persons brought to trial were *conversos*. Though charged with heresy, they usually were convicted not for deviation from Christian doctrine but for reverting to the forms and customs of Judaism. During the second phase, *conversos* and Moriscos (Muslims converted to Christianity) continued to be among the accused, but most were persons accused of being Protestants or sharing the religious beliefs of Martin Luther, the German monk who founded the Protestant movement. Many of the accused were mystics known as *Alumbrados* (Illuminists), who in reality had no association with Lutheranism though they shared some of Lutheran beliefs. The Illuminist movement was quickly suppressed in the 1520s, but the discovery of a few genuine Protestant groups in Valladolid and Seville in the 1550s caused alarm, resulting in about eight hundred suspects being brought before the Inquisition.

No more than a tiny handful of native Spaniards ever became Protestant converts. The principal threat of Protestantism was in northern Europe, where, as we shall see, both Charles V and Philip II waged costly wars to stamp out the heresy. Philip took steps to prevent the infiltration of Protestant beliefs from contacts with northern Europe. A royal decree prohibited Spanish students from studying in foreign universities, even Catholic ones, with a few exceptions. Through censorship and compilation of an Index of forbidden books, the crown and clergy sought to isolate Spain from heretical intellectual influences. The crown imposed severe penalties for introducing books into the country without permission and for circulating any kind of reading material without a license. The Spanish Inquisition compiled its own Index of forbidden books although there was already an Index compiled by the Church in Rome. The Index, enlarged and revised periodically, came to include not only writings by acknowledged heretics, but many other works containing passages that might be interpreted as heretical. While no works of a major Spanish writer were ever placed on the Index, its very existence had an inhibiting effect on writing and scholarship.

The record of the Spanish Inquisition is only part of the history of Christianity in that country in the fifteenth and sixteenth centuries. In that period Spain led the way in the resurgence and revitalization of Roman Catholicism, a movement usually known as the Catholic Reformation or the Counter Reformation. Although Ferdinand and Isabella, especially the latter, having gained a large measure of control over the Church, attempted some reform, much more was accomplished by their successors, Charles V and Philip II. Without making any concessions or changes in matters of doctrine, the crown and the Spanish clergy sought to combat the worldliness, and laxity of discipline in the clergy which were important causes of the Protestant Revolt in northern Europe.

Among the practices crying for reform were absenteeism of the clergy, sometimes the result of the same person holding and enjoying the income from more than one post, and concubinage. (It was reported that in Barcelona twenty percent of the clergy lived with women.) But the most conspicuous inadequacy was the large number of ignorant, even illiterate priests.

While the monarchs and some of the higher clergy initiated and supported some reforms, most of the impetus for the revitalization of religion came from individuals and the founding of new religious orders. The most dynamic and influential of these was the Society of Jesus (Jesuits), founded in 1534 by Ignatius Loyola. It was at first an almost purely Spanish order. The primary interest of the Jesuits was in education—improving the training of the clergy by founding seminaries and carrying on missionary work in Spain and the New World. They were activists, carrying on the struggle against Protestantism and proselyting among non-Christians. Unlike members of earlier religious orders Jesuits were not required to live in monasteries or religious communities.

Another manifestation of the spirit of reform and rejection of wealth and worldliness of the older orders was the Discalced movement. The Discalced (literally "shoeless") ones wore sandals and led lives of piety, prayer, asceticism, and austerity. Outstanding among them was St. Peter of Alcantara (1492–1562) of the Discalced Franciscans, noted for his life of extreme asceticism. He was influential in encouraging the founding of the Discalced Carmelites by St. Teresa of Ávila (1515–1582) and St. John of the Cross (1542–1591). These reformers often encountered opposition from the entrenched interests of the older orders, but they had the support of the crown, in particular Philip II, and the reformed movements grew rapidly.

The Holy Office of the Inquisition assisted in the Catholic Reformation by efforts to reform and educate the Catholic laity. While cases of heresy continued to come before the tribunal, most of those arrested were ordinary Spanish Catholics charged with lesser offenses, which seldom led to severe penalties. The Inquisition concentrated on enforcing respect for the sacred, punishing blasphemy, sacrilege, and scandalous language. Cases involving sexual morality, in particular violations of the sacrament of marriage, were numerous. In combating sins of these sorts the Holy Office was fighting popular attitudes which condoned or ignored the practices it tried to eliminate. Success in changing overall conduct of the people was limited, but there is reason to believe that efforts during the Catholic Reformation educated the laity in better understanding the tenets of the Church.

Because members of the Spanish religious orders had already carried out reforms in their own country they were in a position to take the lead in broader efforts at reform initiated by the papacy. The Jesuits in particular, who took a special oath of allegiance to the Pope, played an important part in the Council of Trent, which defined Catholic dogma, and developed a program of reform for all of Roman Catholicism.

The Muslim subjects of Granada and the Moriscos deserve special mention. As we have seen, in 1492 Ferdinand and Isabella completed the conquest of the kingdom of Granada, thereby bringing a large Muslim minority under the control of Castile. The terms of the treaty of surrender were generous, but for religious and security reasons this early policy of toleration was reversed. There was fear that the Moorish subjects in Granada would collaborate with the Muslim states of North Africa with which the Spanish were engaged in intermittent wars. Moreover, Ferdinand and Isabella and the clergy found it difficult to tolerate an alien religion and an alien culture. In 1499 the monarchs introduced a policy of forcible conversion at the urging of Archbishop Cisneros of Toledo, Isabella's personal confessor and a man of great power and influence. The Muslims, regarding this as a betrayal of a promise, rose in rebellion. After the uprising was suppressed they were given a choice of conversion to Christianity or expulsion. As might be expected, most of them chose to become nominal Christians, but without religious conviction and with almost no understanding of Christian doctrine. In Aragon and Valencia, where there were also large numbers of Muslims, forcible conversions took place.

Mutual intolerance and suspicion between Old Christians and Moriscos increased during the following decades, and in the sixteenth century the aggressive policies of another Muslim people, the Ottoman Turks, only served to heighten tensions.

The Spain of Ferdinand and Isabella 51

Moriscos were suspected, with reason, of engaging in spying and subversive activities on behalf of the Muslim enemies of Spain.

Missionaries made some limited efforts to instruct the Moriscos. The Inquisition occasionally prosecuted them for heresy, but such cases were few since it was acknowledged that Moriscos understood little of doctrine. Arabic continued to be spoken; Morisco women continued to wear Arabic dress and veils; Muslim dietary rules were observed—all the external practices of Islam continued. Most of the Moriscos were poor peasants; some were skilled artisans or traders, restricted from entry into many occupations by purity of blood laws.

In 1576 a decree of Philip II, issued on the recommendation of the clergy, prohibited most Islamic practices, including Arabic dress and the use of the Arabic language, and suppressed most Arabic literature. The next year resentment erupted into a serious revolt centered in the Alpujarras Mountains in Granada. On both sides there was ferocious fighting, though hoped for aid from the Turks and North Africa for the Moriscos did not arrive. The revolt was finally crushed by an army led by Don Juan of Austria, half brother of Philip II. The government's answer to Morisco discontent was forcible removal and resettlement in other parts of Spain. Granada was laid desolate, many of its towns and villages left empty, but some land was repopulated by Old Christians.

In spite of these drastic measures Moriscos remained a largely unassimilated population, while the birthrate among them continued to exceed that of the Old Christians. In 1582, after much deliberation, the crown decided that the only solution lay in a general expulsion, a policy opposed in some places, in particular by the great landowners in Valencia where many Moriscos were tenants. For various reasons there were delays, but finally in 1609, during the reign of Philip III, removal commenced and continued for several years. There are no accurate figures, but many thousands were driven from their homeland. Most of them went to North Africa, but some like

Ricote, the Morisco in *Don Quixote*, went to Christian countries in western Europe.

By the end of the sixteenth century a large degree of religious and ethnic unity had been achieved. In a Europe torn by religious wars between Catholics and Protestants, Spain was a bastion of orthodox Catholicism. This unity had been achieved at a cost to future cultural and material development. The expulsion of Jews and Moriscos was not only a human tragedy but a loss of valuable intellectual talents and skilled workers.

However repugnant the Inquisition to modern standards of religious and intellectual freedom, the cost in human lives was small in comparison to the numbers killed in the religious wars in neighboring France and in the religious wars outside Spain in which Spanish soldiers fought and died under Charles V and Philip II. The years of the Catholic Reformation coincided with and preceded a brilliant era in art and literature, the so-called "Golden Century," and out of that Reformation came missionaries and religious enthusiasm which were important in shaping Hispanic America.

Whatever the success of the religious policies of the crown and Church in Spain, however, in the New World they would encounter different challenges and contradictions. The quest on the Spanish peninsula for racial purity conflicted with colonial realities—there were at first few Spanish women in the New World, and many of the explorers took wives from the Indian female population. Similarly, the quest for religious purity—seen in the expulsion of Jews and Moriscos from Spain—would soon be confronted by countless native Indian religions in Central and South America.

PART III

THE WORLD COLUMBUS DISCOVERED: SPAIN'S BEGINNINGS IN AMERICA

"The greatest event since the creation of the world (excluding the incarnation and death of Him who created it) is the discovery of the Indies," wrote a Spanish historian in 1552, sixty years after the first voyage of Columbus (Gómara, *General History of the Indies,* quoted in Elliott, 10). Christopher Columbus himself, who "discovered" what we usually call the New World, died without realizing that on his first voyage he had reached the outposts of a whole continental system hitherto unknown to Europeans. The fact that the Spanish possessions in the New World were long known as the Indies and the native Americans as Indians shows that Columbus thought that he had reached the outskirts of the Indies in the Far East—the original object of his first voyage. But his voyages ushered in a new era, the foundations of a vast Spanish overseas empire and the beginnings of the transmission of European culture to those new lands.

As is well known, Columbus was a native of Genoa, Italy, and had long cherished a vision of proving the global nature of the earth and reaching the Far East by sailing westward across the Atlantic. He had sailed on Portuguese sponsored expeditions to Africa in the 1480s and was familiar with the growing knowledge about the South Atlantic. Columbus had unsuccessfully sought aid in other quarters—in Portugal, France and England—and had been rebuffed on an earlier visit to Spain. But in 1492, at an auspicious time following the surrender of Granada, he appealed successfully to Queen Isabella, who regarded his expedition as an offering of thanks for victory over the infidel and an opportunity for renewed dedication to the spread of Christianity. The authorization given Columbus was a grant from the crown of Castile under which any lands he might discover would be the possession of Castile. For himself Columbus would receive noble rank, the hereditary title of Admiral of the Ocean Sea, and the right to one tenth of the merchandise and trade of the new lands.

On the first voyage he set out with three small ships and a total crew of ninety. On October 12, 1492 he reached land—a small island in the Bahamas. He also landed on Hispaniola (Santo Domingo) and Cuba, returning to Spain early in 1493 to report to Ferdinand and Isabella.

The second voyage of Columbus, a much more ambitious undertaking than the first, carried more than a thousand men, including twelve priests, as well as horses and livestock and seeds for planting crops. A permanent settlement was made on Hispaniola. On two later voyages Columbus discovered Trinidad and touched on the mainland of South and Central America. For about twenty years Hispaniola and other islands in the West Indies were the focal point for Spanish settlement. The first Spanish city in the New World, Santo Domingo, was founded in 1496, in Hispaniola. Thereafter settlement spread to the mainland, and in 1513 an intrepid explorer, Vasco Núñez de Balboa, crossed the Isthmus of Panama to discover the Pacific Ocean. Six years later Ferdinand Magellan began a voyage which took him across the Pacific and resulted in the first circumnavigation of the earth.

That same year (1519), Hernán Cortés, landing on the coast of Mexico with a small band of men, began a march which resulted in the fall of the Aztec empire. In 1531 Francisco Pizarro set out on an expedition across enormous distances and mountain barriers which ended two years later in the overthrow of the mighty Inca empire.

By 1540 the greatest age of conquest was over—a feat accomplished in a period of less than fifty years by an incredibly small group of men. By that date Spanish settlements were being made over a widespread area and a Hispanic-American

Spain's Beginnings in America

Map 2: Meso-America in the Age of the Conquistadors

culture was taking shape over the remains of conquered native civilizations.

Spectacular as was the achievement of the Spanish, they had not taken the lead in overseas exploration. That distinction belonged to neighboring Portugal. With its long Atlantic coastline and a long maritime tradition it was natural that Portugal should embark upon voyages of exploration, seeking gold, silver, and slaves. Religious motives, to push back Islam in Africa, also impelled the Portuguese. By the time Columbus reached America the Portuguese had reached the Cape of Good Hope at the southern tip of Africa. A few years later Vasco da Gama sailed around the Cape and across to India, demonstrating that there was a feasible all-water route to the Far East. Portugal founded a far flung empire and developed a flourishing trade in Africa and Asia. The empire was primarily commercial, consisting of scattered trading posts and fortresses to control strategic spots along the coasts of Africa and the sea routes to India and the Spice Islands (modern Indonesia). Few settlers went from Portugal to the colonies. While there was some missionary activity, efforts to control and convert native people were limited.

The Spanish were well aware of Portugal's interest in exploration and commerce and were already rivals with her for control of the Canary Islands. To forestall possible Portuguese claims Ferdinand and Isabella asked for and received a papal order recognizing their right to lands they discovered. In 1493 a papal bull confirmed the Spanish title, giving legitimacy from the highest source of Christian authority to their claims. Later, under the Treaty of Tordesillas (1494), a line of demarcation was drawn which gave Spain title to all lands in America except Brazil.

Within a few years, building on models established during the Reconquest, the Spanish established an empire of a very different nature from that of Portugal—an empire intended not merely as a commercial venture but as a Spanish colonial enterprise. But before we turn to the empire let us look at the first encounters of the Spanish explorers with the environment and people of the New World.

Beginnings of Settlement and Cultural Exchange

It is impossible for persons living in an age when men have landed on the moon, when astronauts go regularly on space missions, when television brings the most remote lands and people into our living rooms, to imagine the reaction of the first Europeans to the sights and people of the New World. They themselves were filled with wonder and almost disbelief, and their accounts fired the imagination and widened the intellectual horizons of Europeans who heard or read of their adventures.

Fortunately for posterity, Columbus kept a journal of his first voyage and wrote a long letter to his sponsor, Queen Isabella. There were numerous first-hand accounts by other early explorers, who sometimes had difficulty in finding words to describe birds and animals and human beings so alien to their previous experience. In 1492 Columbus and his crew thought that they had reached islands off the coast of Asia, but they were puzzled by the plants and animals they saw. There were many unfamiliar trees and plants and flowers, but no grapes, so necessary for sacramental wine as well as the customary Spanish drink. There were strange birds, fish and reptiles and no horses or cattle.

But it was the human beings, the native Americans, who most startled and puzzled the Spanish. They had had experience with black Africans and knew something of the peoples of Asia, but the Indians were far more exotic. Columbus was impressed and shocked by the nakedness of the natives he first saw—they apparently had no sense of shame. In describing them and his first encounters with them Columbus wavered in his perception between seeing them as peaceable, innocent creatures ("noble savages") and seeing them as innately cruel brutes. The reactions of Columbus were typical of the early *conquistadores,* whose perceptions of the native peoples were of course based on their own Spanish, Christian values and code of conduct. On the one hand, they reasoned, Indians must be human beings created by God, with immortal souls. One of the purposes of the expedition of Columbus was to spread Christianity. Taking some of the natives back to Spain with him he expressed to Isabella the hope that she would soon make Christians of them and would have them instructed in the "good manners" of her kingdom. But the Spanish also saw the indigenous people as different from themselves and therefore inferior. As Christians they thought that monogamous marriage was ordained by God, and they were shocked by the variety of sexual practices among the Indians. They were unprepared to face the fact of cultural pluralism and thought that the native peoples must be children of the devil—a view which justified enslaving them.

Ambivalence of perception and purpose was apparent from the beginning in the treatment of the native Americans. Priests were brought to Hispaniola on Columbus' second voyage, but in their first encounters the Spanish were often ruthless and cruel. On his return to Europe from the second voyage Columbus carried off four hundred Indians as slaves, of whom two hundred died in route. Indian women were particularly unfortunate. Because there were almost no women on the early expeditions the *conquistadores* permitted their men to carry off women as concubines. From the beginning contact with the Spanish had a disruptive effect on native families and social institutions.

News of Columbus' discoveries spread more quickly to Europe than might have been expected in an age when communication was slow. Popular interest is shown by the fact that his first letter was printed and published nine times in 1493 and had reached some twenty editions by 1500. Accounts of other *conquistadores* and explorers were eagerly seized upon by a reading public which was rapidly growing as the result of the development of printing. The discoveries had an incalculable effect upon European thought. "The very fact of America's existence, and of its gradual revelation as an entity in its own right, constituted a challenge to a whole body of traditional assumptions, beliefs, and attitudes" (Elliott, *The Old World and the New*, 8).

The old authorities of classical antiquity had no knowledge of these new lands. The scientific theories of Christian Europe had been drawn principally from Aristotle and the Bible—and these did not prepare Europeans for the new discoveries. For example, it was difficult to reconcile the existence of hitherto unknown living creatures with the Biblical account of creation. More specifically, it did not seem possible so many varieties could have survived the flood by being herded onto Noah's ark.

The New World opened new vistas for scientific inquiry; it also was the inspiration for much imaginative literature. Among the *conquistadores* themselves there was much fantasizing and romanticizing as they sought elusive, often mythical, realms of gold and fountains of youth. Their tales in turn had a tremendous effect upon literature.

A mixture of motives—religion, greed, and thirst for adventure—impelled Columbus and other early explorers and *conquistadores* to set out on expeditions fraught with danger and uncertainty. Columbus saw his first voyage as part of a divine plan to make Christianity universal. His journal frequently mentioned what he regarded as evidence of divine intervention. The beginning of his journal linked his mission with religious developments in Spain—the conquest of Granada and the expulsion of the Jews. He expressed the hope that the Catholic Monarchs would send priests to convert inhabitants of lands he might reach, "just as your Highnesses destroyed those who were unwilling to confess the Father, the Son, and the Holy Ghost" (quoted in Todorov, 50).

Columbus also frequently mentioned the quest for gold and pursued every hint of the precious metal given by the Indians. Little gold was actually discovered in the islands, but by holding out the prospect of riches he probably hoped to hold the support of the crew and to impress the Catholic Monarchs. He assured Isabella that he hoped that the gold would be used by the crown to spread Christianity. But he was also impelled by the excitement of discovery and adventure. The men who came after Columbus were influenced by similar motives. The thrill of discovery and the ease of conquest gave them the sense of divine mission and enhanced the feeling of Spanish superiority and confidence. As in the Reconquest of Spain from the Muslims, a militant Catholicism pervaded the undertakings. A priest accompanied every expedition, and most places received religious names. As Bernal Díaz, the chronicler of the adventures of Cortés, succinctly expressed it: "We came to serve God and His Majesty and to get rich" (Díaz).

The first arrivals in the New World were mostly unmarried young men, often with some military experience. They were inured to warfare and an arduous life, ready to endure the rigors of a frontier society. Tales of quick riches brought increasing numbers of immigrants from Spain. Although members of the *hidalgo* class furnished much of the leadership of the conquests and early settlements, the largest number of immigrants were from areas of rural poverty. Later more of the urban poor came. Hopes of escaping from the burden of taxation and poor crops and exchanging the struggle for existence in Spain for the greater opportunities of the New World brought them. Most of the immigrants did not become wealthy, but there was greater economic freedom and economic and social mobility in America than in Spain. Some of these who came expected to make their fortunes and return to Spain, and indeed some did, but most of them and their descendants remained in America.

Few women came on the first ships. By the 1550s women made up about fifteen percent of the Spanish population in the colonies; by the end of the century that figure had grown substantially. The absence of white women among the early immigrants led to widespread miscegenation and a racially mixed population.

In the papal bull of demarcation and in regulations issued during the lifetime of Isabella the right to emigrate was limited to Castilians. Later Ferdinand permitted small numbers of Aragonese to leave for America, and in 1596 Philip II confirmed the right of all Spaniards to go. In spite of regulations limiting immigration to persons from Spain, some persons of other nationalities filtered in, often in connection with commerce.

The settlers hoped to create a way of life in their new home patterned on the old. Nowhere was this more evident than in agriculture, with the result that in less than a century a veritable biological revolution had occurred. Three products considered essential by Mediterranean people were wheat for bread, grapes for wine, and olives, all unknown in America. On his second voyage Columbus brought all of these essentials and seeds for other crops as well. By the 1550s wheat had become the most widely cultivated crop in the Spanish colonies. It was not easy to find terrain suitable for vineyards, but grapes were grown successfully in Peru and later in Chile. Sugar cane was already a profitable crop in the Canary Islands and to a lesser extent in Granada. Introduced into Hispaniola by Columbus, sugar growing spread from there to other islands and to Brazil, the Portuguese colony on the mainland. Other fruits and crops grown in Spain, many of which had first been introduced in Europe by Arabs, were now brought to the New World, among them rice, oranges, lemons, and figs. Bananas arrived from the Canary Islands. In turn maize (Indian corn), potatoes, beans, squash, cocoa, and tobacco were taken from America to Europe.

The Spaniards also brought animals. Undoubtedly the most influential in historical development was the horse, an animal unknown to America. Horses enabled the *conquistadores* to travel long distances, extending geographical frontiers. In warfare they were a key factor in making it possible for a handful of Spaniards to defeat vastly larger Indian forces. From Spain the colonists brought animals considered necessary for agriculture—mules, donkeys, oxen, fowl, and dogs. Sheep and cattle, important in Spain, soon grazed on plains and plateaus in America. The introduction of oxen altered methods of cultivation, making it possible to pull plows through soil too heavy for the sticks used by Indians. The exchange of plants and animals between Spain and America eventually produced a large degree of biological homogeneity and blurred differences between the Old World and the New.

During the early years of Spanish settlement *conquistadores* and colonists were primarily interested in seeking quick riches through the discovery of gold and silver. They imported food from Spain before they could supply their own needs, but before long agriculture developed to feed the Spanish settlers and the Indians who labored in the mines. The Spaniards did find gold, but the real "gold mine" proved to be silver. The richest veins of silver yet known were discovered in Mexico and Peru. Silver became for a time the mainstay of the colonial economy and was used to sustain the imperial ventures and wars of Charles V and Philip II in Europe. Mines were developed by private entrepreneurs with some regulation by royal authorities and the requirement that a certain share (the royal fifth) be paid to the crown. Some have argued that the silver brought back to Spain from the New World transformed the currencies of Europe and fundamentally altered the European economy.

By the end of the sixteenth century mining as a source of quick wealth was declining as the richest veins of silver were exhausted. Meanwhile farming and raising cattle and sheep were expanding to become the basis for the colonial economy. For these enterprises, as well as for construction of cities and the transport of goods, the Spaniards needed labor—labor that the native Americans were expected to furnish.

Spaniards and Native Americans

Isolated geographically for thousands of years by two oceans, native Americans had developed their own institutions and cultures, free from outside influences. For them the appearance of Europeans, the shock of invasion by human beings so strange and different, was traumatic.

The Spanish explorers and settlers left many written accounts describing the New World and its inhabitants, and these are complemented by a lesser number of Indian accounts. At first oral communication between the two groups was almost non-existent, which limited enormously their capacity for mutual understanding. Many among the Aztecs initially viewed the Spaniards as gods. The Aztecs possessed a complex cosmology and Cortés resembled the description of one of their principal gods, Quetzalcoatl. Moreover, Cortés and his men arrived in the first year of a 52-year cycle in the Aztec calendar, just when the prophecies had foretold the return of Quetzalcoatl. Yet it was not long before some Indians grew suspicious of the Spaniards and abandoned the view of the explorers as divine visitors.

There were wide variations and diversity in the cultures, languages, and degrees of material progress among the native Americans whom the Spanish encountered. The natives of the first islands discovered and settled lived a simple existence, planting necessary foodstuffs, fishing, and sometimes panning for small amounts of gold from the streams. In contrast, on the mainland Cortés and Pizarro found highly developed and complex civilizations, the mighty empires of the Aztecs and the Incas.

The empire Cortés encountered, a conglomeration of states and languages covering an area roughly coterminous with modern Mexico, had been conquered and subdued by the Aztecs only a few generations before the arrival of the Spaniards. The sight of the magnificent capital city, Tenochtitlan, with its immense stone buildings and huge sculptures, evidence of architectural and engineering skills, filled the Spaniards with amazement. Later they learned that the Aztecs had developed a pictographic system of writing and kept many records, most of which the invaders destroyed. The Aztecs had armies, an elaborate system of administration, and considerable internal trade. Farm tools were primitive, but a variety of food crops was raised, as was cotton from which cloth for textiles was woven. Iron was not known; most tools, arrowheads, and weapons were made of stone, but some were made of bronze. Silver and gold were mined. The Spaniards were dazzled and their greed whetted by the sight of ornaments and utensils made from the precious metals. On all sides were signs of religion and religious ceremonies, including some evidences of human sacrifice, which horrified the invaders.

The Inca empire in what is now Peru, named for the supreme ruler whose subjects believed him to be divine, had been in existence less than a century when Pizarro appeared. The Inca state and economy were a unique regimented system, a kind of state socialism. Religion was also highly organized with numerous priesthoods and temples to the Sun. Buildings showed a high level of architectural and engineering skills. The economy, based on agriculture, produced maize, white and sweet potatoes, squash, beans, tomatoes, peanuts, and cocoa. The Andean societies had achieved notable skills in textile weaving.

We still do not know with certainty how it was possible for a mere handful of Spaniards, a few thousand at most, to conquer these vast empires and subdue the populations in so short a time. Several factors were partly responsible. One was the obvious discrepancy in weaponry. The Indians were without firearms and cannon. In a sense it was the world of iron and gunpowder against the stone age. Arrowheads and hatchets could not compete with guns. In fact, however, the Spanish had relatively few firearms though what they had terrified the Indians. They had the advantage of metal swords and pikes as well as metal helmets which Indian arrows and hatchets could not penetrate. Perhaps more terrifying and demoralizing than firearms were the horses which the Spaniards rode and the savage dogs which they set against the Indians. In addition, internal conditions in both the Aztec and Inca empires weakened resistance. Bitterness of native states against conquest and domination by their Aztec and Inca rulers caused some to cooperate actively with the Spanish or remain passive. There were also intangible, psychological factors which cannot be measured. There were Indian myths and prophesies foretelling invasions by white gods, but their importance in influencing Indian behavior is difficult to estimate. The Spanish were supremely confident, convinced that theirs was a mission with a divine blessing. Their amazingly easy victories strengthened their confidence. In contrast, the native Americans often appeared to be fatalistic, although some of them fought fiercely.

Whatever the reasons for the ease of the early military victories, the effects of invisible killers, epidemics of disease, were in the long run far more disastrous than warfare to the native population. Although epidemics continued to take massive tolls of life in Europe, over the centuries those who survived developed, if not total immunity, at least resistance to certain diseases. On the other hand, the native Americans had never been exposed to such diseases as measles, tuberculosis, and smallpox before the arrival of the Europeans. The result was a catastrophic decline in population, particularly during the first decades of contact between Indians and Spaniards. The pages of the accounts of the early empire are full of references to the susceptibility of the natives to disease and the appalling number of deaths. By the 1580s as the result of disease and Spanish brutality the native population of the islands was almost extinct, while on parts of the mainland the population had declined by as much as 90 percent. There has been no comparable depopulation of an entire cultural region in all of world history.

Epidemics sometimes affected the ability of native Americans to offer more effective resistance to the *conquistadores.* During the campaign of Cortés the Aztecs had resisted the first attack on Tenochtitlan and had forced the Spaniards to withdraw and regroup before further attack. In the words of one chronicler, "When the Christians were exhausted from war, God saw fit to send the Indians smallpox, and there was a great pestilence in the city" (quoted in Crosby, 48). Had there been no outbreak of the disease the Aztec warriors might successfully have pursued the invaders. Their numbers and capacity to fight were sapped by the epidemic and the city, besieged by the returning Spanish, surrendered. It was several generations before Indian numbers began to increase again, as descendants of those few who survived the original onslaught and acquired immunity intermarried among themselves or with persons of Spanish ancestry.

From the first encounters the Spaniards were of at least two minds in their perception and treatment of the native Americans, and as time went on the gap between theory and reality widened. On the one hand, one of the avowed purposes of exploration and conquest was to spread Christianity. But the appearance and habits of the natives, so exotic and sometimes shocking, repelled the *conquistadores* and raised doubts in their minds as to whether they were indeed members of the human race, subject to conversion and salvation. More important, most of the *conquistadores* and early settlers were intent on quick riches, and they needed the Indians as laborers.

In contrast, the missionaries who followed in the wake of the explorers and sometimes accompanied them were committed to the conversion and education of the natives. In principle the position of the crown and the clergy coincided. Queen Isabella saw the Indians as subjects of the crown, to be Christianized and protected, and opposed their enslavement. She sent back to Hispaniola some of those whom Columbus brought back as slaves on his second voyage. In the eyes of the monarchs Spain conquered and ruled in America by the authority of the Pope. Every military commander was instructed to read a statement justifying their subjection to Spanish rule to the uncomprehending Indians. It declared that all men were brothers and that the world had been divided by the Pope, the direct representative of God, between the rulers of Castile and Portugal so that Indians might be converted to the faith.

During the sixteenth century members of the religious orders represented a powerful force opposed to enslavement and exploitation. One of the great enterprises of the Roman Catholic Church was the missionary work of Spanish priests in the New World. Their endeavors represented the greatest expansion of Christianity since the early Middle Ages. Thousands of monks and priests came to the New World, in part to serve the religious needs of the Spanish settlers, but primarily to convert and educate the native Americans.

Members of the Franciscan order had arrived early in Hispaniola and large numbers came to Mexico in 1524. Dominicans and Augustinians were also numerous, and later in the sixteenth century Jesuits arrived. For these missionaries America offered an opportunity to found a Christian society uncontaminated by the corruption and worldliness of Old Europe. Looking upon the natives as "noble savages," most of them wanted to protect their liberty and bring them voluntarily into the Church, although there were examples of forced conversions. In the process of conversion and education the missionaries, however idealistic their motives, were seeking to eliminate native religions and cultures. In this they appeared to have spectacular success, but in most cases the conversions were in reality superficial. Beneath the veneer of Christianity pagan beliefs and practices survived.

The Spanish monarchs, concerned with Christianizing and protecting the Indians though they were, nevertheless saw the New World as a source of wealth, wealth that could be obtained only through the enterprise of white settlers and the labor of the Indians.

The result was the *encomienda,* a system adapted from practices developed during the Reconquest. In Spain grants of land had been made by the rulers in return for military assistance and to encourage settlement. In the New World, first in Hispaniola, later on the mainland, it was not the land which was allotted but the Indians, in groups called *encomiendas.* In return for their labor the Spanish recipient, the *encomendero,* had an obligation to protect them and to instruct them in Christianity. Whatever the intention of Isabella, who first authorized it, the system was obviously subject to abuse, becoming immediately cruel and exploitative. Slavery was theoretically prohibited, but there was little difference between slavery and the forced labor in the *encomienda.*

As early as 1510 Dominicans in Hispaniola denounced the labor system. The best known and most effective critic was a Dominican, Bartolomé de las Casas. As a result of his influence Emperor Charles V announced New Laws in 1542 which decreed the abolition of the *encomienda* and the liberation of Indian slaves. Earlier in 1512 Ferdinand had issued the Laws of Burgos forbidding the exploitation of Indians, but they had had little effect. The laws of Charles also proved unenforceable in Peru, where efforts to abolish forced labor caused a revolt by the whites. Later Las Casas was permitted to publish *The Destruction of the Indies* in which he assailed the entire history of the Spanish conquest for its cruelty and ruthlessness.

Ironically, as a protection to the Indians, who were threatened with extermination, Las Casas proposed the importation of African slaves as a labor force, a proposal which he later regretted. But as early as 1518 licenses were issued for the importation of black slaves, and as available Indian labor diminished, large numbers were brought to the Spanish islands and to parts of the mainland.

The *encomenderos'* efforts to make themselves into a hereditary aristocracy, through the labor of the Indians allotted to them, were thwarted not so much by the decrees of Charles V as by the decline of the native population. Gradually the *encomienda* was replaced by the *hacienda,* which survived for centuries. As the Indian population disappeared the Spanish were able to take over large tracts of land and make them into private estates worked by leased or contract labor. A similar labor system developed for the mines. While it was less conspicuously ruthless and exploitative than the *encomienda,* Indians continued to live lives of abject poverty. In addition to the labor which they owed to their masters Indians were required to pay taxes to the state and ecclesiastical dues, which contributed to making the Church the wealthiest institution in the New World.

Government and Society in the Colonies

In the space of a few years, the *conquistadores* had expanded the authority of Spain (or more precisely, of the crown of Castile) over a vast territorial empire and a large native population. The conquest was not carried out directly by the crown, which lacked the necessary resources. Public and private initiatives combined, following the precedent of the Reconquest and the settlement of the Canary Islands. Expeditions were sent out under the terms of *capitulaciones,* contracts between crown and military leaders under which lands were to be taken and governed under the authority of the crown, which was also guaranteed a share of the wealth which might be brought back. In return the *conquistadores* were promised rewards from the spoils of conquest and privileges, often hereditary titles of nobility.

Both monarchs and settlers intended that the new lands should be made a replica of old Spain. As in the Reconquest, settlements were made by groups, rather than by individuals. As in the Spanish tradition all persons were identified as residents of a community. Sites for towns and cities were selected for economic and strategic reasons—on good harbors, fertile valleys, near mines, or at points that afforded defense against Indians. Some, like Mexico City, were built on the ruins of large native cities, others on sites previously uninhabited. The ancient Roman tradition of cities laid out on a rectangular pattern was revived. The Laws of the Indies issued by the crown gave precise instructions for the founding of a town, stipulating that "every city in Spanish America should evoke wonder in the Indians when they saw it so that they would thereby understand that the Spanish were permanently settled and, accordingly, should be feared and respected, their friendship sought, and no offense to be given" (quoted in Picón-Salas, 44).

As in towns and cities in Spain, there was an urban center in which all citizens lived, including *encomenderos* who had estates in the country. Around a central plaza stood the church, the municipal building, the *casa real* in which representatives of the crown met, and shops and markets. A periphery of land around the town was allotted to settlers for cultivation. There were also common lands for grazing, cutting wood, etc. All settlements, even small frontier towns as well as cities, followed this pattern. The towns were planned for the Spanish settlers, but some Indians as well as *mestizos* lived within their borders. Indian villages lay in the hinterlands, beyond the municipal boundaries.

As in Spain a stratified social system developed, one which reflected the racial mix of the population. At the top was a small group of *peninsulares,* of pure Spanish blood, born in Spain, usually officials or bureaucrats appointed by the crown. Beneath them were the *criollos,* persons of white Spanish ancestry born in America, who controlled much of the land and wealth and resented the privileged position claimed by the *peninsulares.* Below the *criollos* were persons of mixed racial ancestry. Most numerous were *mestizos* of white and Indian ancestry. Mulattoes were of white and African descent. In a society where there were few white women miscegenation between white men and Indian women was widespread in the early years and often occurred in later years. At the bottom of the social pyramid were pure-blooded Indians, technically free but constituting an oppressed peasant class, and blacks, most of whom were slaves. Zambos were a mixture of Indian and African blood. Persons of mixed blood, *mestizos* in particular, occupied an intermediate status, not entirely accepted by either the white or Indian community, but playing an indispensable role in the economy as skilled artisans, overseers on large estates, and foremen in the mines. Although we see here a social hierarchy based partially upon race, it is important to note the frequency of intermarriage and the subtle gradations in racial classification that this produced, both of which stand in marked contrast to early racial attitudes in most of the United States. Here again we see a legacy of traditional Spanish culture, with its long history of racial mixing (although this had been curtailed in recent years).

After the initial conquests the crown sought to bring the colonies under royal control by establishing an elaborate system of officials and administration entirely subordinate to the monarchy, with no system of checks and balances. In 1525 a Council of the Indies was set up in Spain with supreme authority. There were no representative bodies in the New World like the *cortes* in the Spanish kingdoms. At the apex of royal authority in the colonies was the governor or viceroy. A law issued by Charles V said the colonies were to be "ruled and governed by viceroys who represent our royal person." Because of the prestige attached to the office and the possibilities for financial gain, it was eagerly sought. Appointments always went to members of the upper nobility but only ones on whose complete loyalty the monarch could depend. Viceroys often found their position frustrating, burdened as they were by lengthy instructions from Spain that were often impossible to follow.

Beneath the viceroy was the *audiencia,* a council appointed by the crown with both administrative and judicial functions. Below them was an elaborate bureaucracy. The higher officers usually came from Spain, partly to emphasize royal authority but also to provide career opportunities for office seekers. Some appointees bought their offices, and there was a tendency for all bureaucrats to use the years served in America to make as much money as they could from the local community before returning home.

There is much reason to believe that the elaborate system of colonial administration in which all authority stemmed from the crown existed on paper, but that actual operation was in reality quite different. In fact some scholars have concluded that centralized control by the Spanish government was illusory. In the first place, there was the space-time obstacle. Distances between Spain and the New World were great; travel was exceedingly slow and time consuming. Modern methods of communication were of course non-existent. Delays in communication hindered decision-making and frustrated action. Months elapsed between the time a policy decreed in the Council of the Indies was even known in America, far less carried out. Actual conditions in America often made it impractical to implement royal policie.

Slowness of communication hindered decisive action to defend the colonies against outside attack. For example, when the English marauder, Sir Francis Drake, raided the city of Santo Domingo in 1586, Philip II did not learn of it for three months—too late to take effective counteraction. In any event, Spain had virtually no naval or land forces in the New World. Nearly all her manpower and resources were used to fight the wars of Charles V and Philip II in Europe. Under the circumstances real control in the colonies passed to a large extent to the American elite, the *criollos*.

If political control by the crown was limited, the power of the Church, the wealthiest institution in the New World, was very great, and the Church was directly under the power of the Spanish monarchy. In return for their efforts at converting the natives the Pope had granted the rulers of Castile sole control over appointments and collection of church revenues. Bishops appointed by the crown were in effect royal functionaries, playing an important part in civil as well as religious life. At the local level parish churches founded primarily for the Spanish settlers were the keystone of ecclesiastical organization.

By the end of the sixteenth century the idealism and evangelical zeal of the early days of the Church in America had declined. Most of the missionaries had been moved to the frontier. Mission churches continued to serve the Indians, but in the towns and cities, which were the centers of power, the lower clergy, like the bishops, were identified with royal authority and the social ascendancy of the colonial elite. By preaching loyalty and obedience to Church and state to *mestizos* and Indians they helped to maintain social stability.

During the early years, through the work of missionary members of the religious orders, there had been apparently spectacular progress in the conversion of native Americans to Christianity. Overt evidences of earlier Indian religions virtually disappeared. In Mexico, for example, friars eliminated certain aspects of Aztec religion—the temples, the priests, and human sacrifice. Among Indians generally the visible parts of Christianity were those most readily embraced—the ceremonies, the processions, the images of the saints. In Indian religions there were analogies to some aspects of Christian practices, including marriage, penance, baptism, and fasting. Indian acceptance of these was colored by their earlier beliefs and hence interpreted differently by Indians and priests. For example, the community of saints of the Catholics was received by the Indians as a pantheon of anthropomorphic deities. The Christian God was accepted but not in a monotheistic sense. As usually happens when there are mass conversions to a new religion, there was little understanding of doctrine or theology. The Roman Catholicism of the native population was a syncretism of the old and new.

In the New World as in Spain, Church and state were united in efforts to stamp out heresy and blasphemy. After a few isolated accusations against *converso* immigrants and Lutherans, Philip II secured the establishment of an independent tribunal of the Inquisition in Mexico City in 1569 for the purpose of "freeing the land, which had been contaminated by Jews and heretics." Most of the persons first brought before the court were English Lutherans who had landed in Spanish territory after unsuccessful attacks on Spanish treasure ships. Thereafter most of the accused were Protestants, who for trade or other reasons were within Spanish jurisdiction, and *conversos,* most frequently from Portugal. By 1601 almost nine hundred trials had taken place. Another Inquisition was established in Lima and later tribunals in other cities. The Inquisition usually did not have jurisdiction over Indians, though there were a few cases. Indians were regarded as not sufficiently educated in Christianity to be knowingly guilty of heresy. In 1571 all jurisdiction over Indians was removed from the Inquisition and placed under the bishops.

Churches, cathedrals, monasteries, and convents built with some of the wealth of the Church were visible evidences of its greatness. The Cathedrals, begun soon after the arrival of the first settlers, were among the grandest and most impressive in Christendom. Outside they were decorated with sculptures and elaborate carvings; inside were gilded ceilings, altars covered with gold leaf, and polychrome sculptures. The churches were in a sense symbols of the fusion of Hispanic and native cultures. The cathedral in Mexico City rose on the site of the principal pyramid temple of the Aztecs. A Christian church was erected on the site of the temple of the Sun in Cuzco in Peru. Indeed, the placement of cathedrals and churches on the sites of former Indian temples was a physical symbol of the conquest of Indian religions by Catholicism. Yet, as with the syncretism that became evident in religious practice, some motifs of earlier Indian art were visible in the carvings that decorated churches built by Indian labor.

Schools and universities modeled on those of Spain were founded very early by the religious orders to train colonists for the clergy and to give a more general education to the *criollos* and a few *mestizos.* One of the avowed purposes of the missionaries was to educate as well as to convert the Indians. But in fact the Indian masses and most of the *mestizos* remained untaught and illiterate. Students in the Dominican and Jesuit schools received a traditional Hispanic education.

In 1538 the first university in the New World was founded in the first city, Santo Domingo, but as population shifted away from the islands it declined and was closed. The first permanent university was the University of Mexico, chartered in 1551. A university was chartered at Lima the same year but did not actually begin operation for some twenty years. The universities, modeled on the medieval universities in Spain, were established to insure a trained clergy, the foundation upon which colonial culture rested. Theology was the center of the curriculum but courses in medicine and other subjects were also taught.

Within twenty years after the conquest a printing press was introduced in Mexico City, and presses were soon operating in other cities. Books on astronomy, medicine, philosophy, grammar, and vocabularies of native languages were published as well as works on theology. A great variety of books was also imported from Spain.

A Hispanic-American society, not a replica of Old Spain, developed in the colonies. Spanish institutions and culture were superimposed on native cultures fragmented and weakened, but not destroyed by the conquest. The degree of acculturation among the native Americans varied. The Indian chieftains and *mestizos* were like the Spanish in language, customs, clothing, and the food they ate. The mass of Indians continued to speak native languages, wear native costumes, and eat the traditional Indian foods. The Spanish succeeded in making their language the language of government and the upper classes, but interspersed in the vocabulary brought from Spain were Indian words.

Conquest and partial Hispanization were accomplished at a tremendous human cost, but the ruthlessness and destruction do not obscure the dramatic and far-reaching changes which occurred. Within less than a century the invasion of the New World by Spain had drastically altered plant and animal ecology, human demography, government, language, the economy, and religion. The Hispanic-American culture which resulted has survived to the present, not as an unchanging entity, but rather one that continues to struggle with internal tensions and contradictions. The clash of cultures that began in the 1490s is still going on today.

Spain's Beginnings in America

The labor of the enslaved and exploited natives produced wealth which supported the *criollos,* the cost of colonial government, and the Church. But much of that wealth went to Spain to help build magnificent churches and royal palaces, to pay for other luxuries of the monarchy and nobility, but, most of all, to pay for the wars of Charles V and Philip II in Europe.

PART IV

SPAIN UNDER THE EARLY HABSBURGS

Charles V and Philip II

In 1517 the man who was to be known in history as Charles V (Carlos I to his Spanish subjects) arrived in Spain. The child of Juana (Joanna), the daughter of Ferdinand and Isabella, and Philip, Duke of Burgundy, the son of Emperor Maximilian of Austria, he had been born in Ghent in the Netherlands, where he had spent his entire childhood. This was his first visit to Spain. At the age of twenty-six he came to claim the thrones of Castile and Aragon on the death of his grandfather, Ferdinand. He and his mother were proclaimed joint rulers of Castile, but Juana, who had early shown signs of mental illness, never really ruled although she lived until 1555.

Less than two years after his arrival in Spain Charles received news of the death of his paternal grandfather, Maximilian, and hastened off to claim the throne of Austria, his Habsburg inheritance. Thus he became ruler of a vast empire in Europe and America, an empire acquired through inheritance, much of it the result of dynastic marriages arranged between members of royal families to increase their realms and strengthen their power. His European empire was a sprawling agglomeration of people of different languages and cultures, held together by the person of the emperor, and, at the beginning of his reign by a common religion, Roman Catholicism. There was no central administration; each realm was governed by its own institutions and laws.

From his grandmother, Isabella, he inherited the throne of Castile and its possessions in America, where the great era of conquest was just beginning; from Ferdinand the crown of

Aragon, which included Sicily, Sardinia, Naples, and some outposts in North Africa. From his father he had already inherited the Burgundian possessions, the most important of which was the Netherlands (modern Holland and Belgium). From his grandfather, Maximilian, came the title to possessions of the Habsburg family, principally Austria. Finally he was elected Holy Roman Emperor. The Holy Roman Empire, so-called because it was in theory a universal empire, descended from the Roman Empire and blessed by God, was in reality a collection of small states embracing an area roughly equivalent to modern Germany. The emperor, elected by certain of the rulers of these states, had usually been a Habsburg.

Given the personal nature of his empire, Charles needed to be present in each realm to insure his authority and to preserve the loyalty of his subjects. But it was inevitable, given the vastness and diversity of his imperial responsibilities, that he be an absentee monarch of Spain during much of his reign.

Faced with a revolt following his first departure, he returned to Spain in 1522 and spent seven years there, perhaps the most successful of his reign. During this period he married his cousin, the beautiful Princess Isabella of Portugal. Like his grandparents, the Catholic Monarchs, he won the loyalty of his Spanish subjects by traveling from city to city. There was no fixed capital. As King of Spain he tried to carry out some judicial and administrative reforms, but internal affairs were always of secondary importance to imperial. Foreign policy and wars dominated most of his reign. After 1529 he was in Spain only for short periods and at one time was absent for fourteen years. During his absence his wife, Queen Isabella, acted as regent until her death in 1539, when Prince Philip (later Philip II) became regent.

Charles' wars were not wars of conquest but wars fought to carry out what he regarded as his supreme mission, the maintenance of Christian unity in Europe in the face of Lutheran heresy and the "containment" of the Ottoman Turks, Muslim infidels. His Spanish subjects sympathized with these objectives,

Spain Under the Early Habsburgs

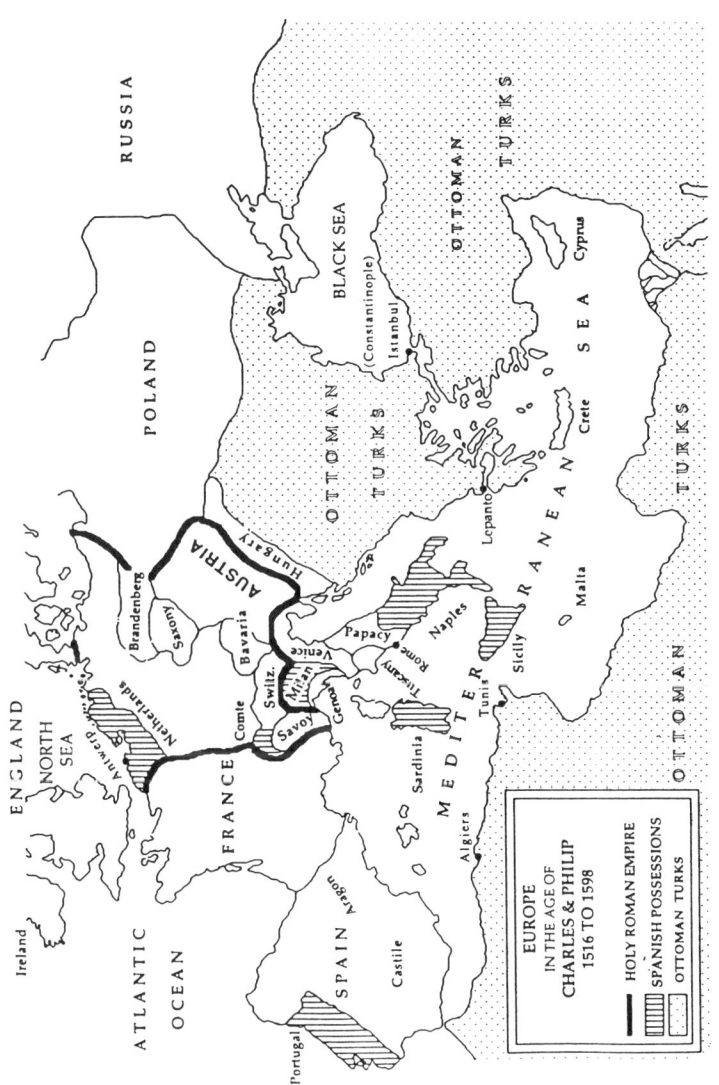

Map 3: Europe 1516-1598

but they also understood that his imperial commitments could threaten the national interests of Spain and diminish their resources. They resented his long absences. As the Admiral of Castile wrote to him:

> Your majesty's protracted absence from your Spanish kingdom, though indispensable perhaps for the safety of threatened Christendom and the furtherance of your political views, is a thing to which your Spanish subjects can hardly reconcile themselves
>
> (quoted in Lynch, 64).

In 1555, wearied and discouraged by failure to achieve his objectives, he abdicated, leaving the government to younger men. To Philip, his oldest child, he bequeathed his Spanish possessions and the Netherlands, the part of the empire where he had been born and which he cherished most. His decision to combine the Spanish heritage and the Netherlands was not merely out of sentiment—there were important economic ties between the two parts of his realm. Located at the confluence of important trade routes, possessing a merchant fleet and prosperous industry, the Netherlands were the most flourishing part of his empire. His Austrian possessions and the title of Holy Roman Emperor went to his younger brother, Ferdinand.

Without question Charles was the strongest influence shaping the career of his son Philip. Instructions which he prepared for him at the time of his first regency in Spain show the values and code of conduct of both father and son. Charles admonished Philip to serve God, uphold the Inquisition, suppress heresy, and never to give an inch of territory but preserve the inheritance given by God—advice which was to lead to disastrous results in the Netherlands. There was a basic continuity in foreign policy between the two rulers, but Philip, without the Austrian inheritance and the Holy Roman Empire, was a much more thoroughly Spanish ruler than his father. After returning to Spain in 1559 he never again left the Iberian Peninsula.

Philip was married four times—twice before his accession to the throne. His first marriage was to Marie, the infanta of Portugal, who died in childbirth, leaving a son, Don Carlos, who was heir apparent. Later he married Mary Tudor, Queen of England, a staunch Catholic, eleven years his senior, as part of a plan of Charles V to bring England into the orbit of Spanish influence. After Mary died childless and after his return to Spain, Philip married Elizabeth of Valois, daughter of the King of France, a girl of fifteen, as part of a peace settlement with France. His last wife was Ana of Austria, twenty-two years his junior, who in six years bore six children, dying in childbirth with the sixth. Philip's first child, Don Carlos, early showed signs of mental instability and irresponsible conduct. He finally was accused of plotting against his father, was arrested, and died in confinement. Philip's only other male heirs were four sickly sons born to Ana of Austria, of whom only one survived, to become Philip III.

Under Philip II Spain reached the apex of its power and entered upon the era often called the Golden Century (*Siglo de Oro*). In Europe his reign was extended over Portugal to which he had a good claim through his mother. When there was a vacancy on the throne his troops marched in and took possession (1586). In the New World Mexico and Peru had been conquered during the reign of Charles. During Philip's reign Spain's rule was spreading to the southwestern part of present day United States and to the Argentine in South America. In the Far East Spanish control over the Philippines was firmly established. With the annexation of Portugal Philip hoped to make his power in the Atlantic supreme.

Often called "Philip the Prudent," he was hard working with an almost overwhelming sense of duty. He was completely devoted to his subjects for whom he felt directly responsible to God. He was devoutly religious, seeking divine guidance for every decision and relying heavily on members of the clergy as ministers and advisors. As monarch he felt he could not display ordinary emotions or signs of weakness. Devoted as he was to his subjects, he was more remote from them than his grandparents and father had been. He abandoned the custom of holding court in different cities, establishing Madrid as his capital. At the royal court he kept a retinue of courtiers from the nobility who performed menial services for him. Every court function was an elaborate ceremony.

Philip's rule is often spoken of as an "absolute monarchy," but the concept of absolutism was far from a political reality. In the first place, a large part of Spain was not directly under royal jurisdiction but was still controlled by great lords whose holdings included hundreds of towns and villages. To govern, the monarch had to rely on the cooperation of the great nobles and the cities. He lacked administrative machinery; there was really no civil service.

The greatest challenge to his authority came from the kingdom of Aragon, where there had always been powerful *cortes* and an aristocracy jealous of their privileges. In Aragon lords had greater power over tenants than in any other part of Philip's realm. After a complex chain of events, including defiance of his authority by certain lawless nobles and an attempt at armed rebellion, in 1592 the king finally resorted to force to restore order, an action which was welcomed by townspeople and many of the nobles. As a result a new constitution was adopted for Aragon which increased the authority of the monarch, giving him more power to protect his subjects.

Philip's last years were unhappy ones for him and for Spain. Discouraged by military defeats and financial crises, bereft of wife and children, suffering from gout and other maladies, he liked to withdraw from court life to El Escorial, the somber monastery-palace which he had built outside of Madrid. There he lived a solitary, austere life, spending hours in the chapel, kneeling in meditation.

Foreign Policies and Wars

Charles V spent most of his reign outside of Spain fighting wars on several fronts. We cannot attempt to follow the diplomatic maneuvering and the military campaigns of Charles and Philip but will simply look at their foreign policy and wars in broad outline.

France was a traditional rival and enemy of the Aragonese kingdom. Ferdinand had used diplomacy and war successfully to check France in Italy. Under his successors hostilities with France continued, and frequently France was involved, either openly or behind the scenes, in the wars of Philip and Charles in the Mediterranean and northern Europe. Both monarchs tried to isolate France diplomatically, and their recurring wars with her drained their resources. But France was not central to the avowed aims of the Spanish Habsburgs.

The two challenges which dominated foreign and military policies were the expansion of Islam in the Mediterranean under the Ottoman Turks and the Protestant Revolt in northern Europe. The costly wars which resulted were religiously motivated (orthodoxy and the religious zeal of Charles and Philip being the basic causes of the struggles), but they were also fought for political and economic power.

The Turks, a people from central Asia converted to Islam during the period of the Arab caliphate in Persia, had gradually extended control over much of the eastern Mediterranean and in 1453, to the consternation of Christendom, had conquered Constantinople. During the reign of Charles V the Turks became more aggressive in the western Mediterranean, threatening Spanish possessions in Italy and North Africa, attacking Spanish ships, and arousing fears that they would foment uprisings among the Morisco population in Spain itself. They were allied with and supported the small Muslim states in North Africa. Charles himself led a successful expedition to Tunis, but a later expedition against Algiers was a failure. Meanwhile the Turks were expanding northward in the Balkan Peninsula and Spanish troops were sent to check their advance toward Hungary. On the whole Charles' efforts against the Turks were ineffectual. Deterioration of Christian power in the western Mediterranean continued.

The inability to stop the Turkish advance in the Mediterranean was due in part to the increasing involvement of Spain in northern Europe. The Protestant Revolt, which shattered the Christian unity of western Europe, began in

Germany, a part of the Holy Roman Empire. The catalyst for the revolt against the authority of the Roman Catholic Church was Martin Luther, an Augustinian monk. His break with Rome was partly the result of his own inner religious experience, which led him to question some aspects of church doctrine, but the immediate cause was his protest over the worldly practices and venality of some members of the Catholic clergy, in particular the sale of indulgences, which were represented as a promise of partial remission of punishment for some sins. Luther's excommunication in 1520 for refusal to recant on this issue was followed by a complete break with Rome and the establishment of a new church. Lutheranism retained much of Roman Catholic doctrine and practice but denied the authority of Rome and the papacy. The religious controversy soon took on political overtones. Some of the German princes, resentful of the domination of the Habsburgs, embraced the new faith and protected Luther and his followers.

In 1529 Charles V came to Germany to settle the matter. He accepted as authority the interpretation of doctrine by Catholic theologians and ordered the princes who protested (hence the term "Protestants") to submit or face the use of force. Finally, all efforts at compromise having failed, Charles declared war on the Protestant princes and brought Spanish and Italian troops into Germany to settle what the princes regarded as a purely domestic matter, thus causing greater dissension. Peace between the contending forces was finally made in 1555. Under the terms of the agreement (made by the Diet of Augsburg) Protestant princes gained equal rights with Catholic rulers to practice their religious beliefs and protect their adherents in their kingdoms. The necessity of coming to terms with the princes and giving recognition to what he regarded as heresy so troubled Charles that it was undoubtedly one of the reasons for his decision to abdicate.

The progress of Lutheranism and its alliance with politics in Germany made him fearful of the spread of heresy in his Netherlands possessions. On his own authority, without papal sanction, he issued various decrees against Lutheranism. After 1550 the death penalty was decreed for all heresy. The policy of

Charles toward England was motivated in part by religion but by political considerations as well, including his concern over the Netherlands. He hoped to extend Habsburg influence over England by the marriage of Philip to Mary Tudor, a step which might lead to the reestablishment of Catholicism in that country and associate it with the defense of the Netherlands. In this, as in his other plans to eliminate Protestantism, he failed.

In foreign affairs Philip II followed the same basic policy as his father, one in which religious and dynastic considerations were dominant. Philip was said to have told his ambassador to Rome that rather than compromise on religion he would choose to lose his dominions and sacrifice his life, because he did not "wish to be lord over heretics." But while he tried to carry out the policy bequeathed by Charles he was unable to draw upon German bankers and German manpower as had his father, but had instead to rely only on the resources of Spain and its possessions and the Netherlands. Like his father he had a dual commitment—against the Turks in the Mediterranean and against Protestantism and revolt in his possessions in northern Europe.

During the first years of his reign affairs in the Mediterranean took priority. From the powerful navy of the Ottoman Empire, Philip faced the same threats as those against which his father had fought without success. In the early years, with inferior naval power, his forces fared badly. In 1560 they suffered a disastrous defeat in North Africa, losing ships and at least ten thousand men taken as prisoners. Thereafter Philip concentrated his resources on building a strong navy which would enable him to take the initiative in the western Mediterranean, where he won a victory off the island of Malta.

Thereafter the center of action shifted to the east. In 1570 a Turkish force landed on the island of Cyprus, a valuable possession of Venice, which had long been a naval and commercial power in the eastern Mediterranean. In response to a plea from the Pope, Philip joined in an alliance with Venice and the papacy against Islam. Spain made the greatest contribution of ships, men and supplies to the naval expedition which followed. Don Juan, Philip's illegitimate half-brother, was put in command. The Christian forces met the Turkish fleet in the Bay of Lepanto off the coast of Greece—208 Christian ships against 230 Turkish galleys. With sacred banners flying on both sides, the battle began. The Christian allies won an overwhelming victory but a costly one in loss of ships and men.

The Ottoman Empire remained intact; Cyprus continued under Turkish control; the Turkish ships were soon replaced. But Lepanto had shown that the Turks were not invincible. Thereafter they were more hesitant about operating in the western Mediterranean. Confrontation between Christendom and Islam subsided, leaving Philip free to turn his attention away from the Mediterranean to northern Europe.

The Netherlands, already in revolt against Spanish rule, became the focal point for Philip's military efforts in a long struggle which proved disastrous for Spain's economic interests. Like the rest of his empire at the beginning of the reign of Charles V, the Netherlands had been solidly Roman Catholic. After the rise of Lutheranism, as we have seen, Charles had taken severe measures to prevent its spread. In the Netherlands, Protestantism came in three forms. Lutheranism infiltrated to several areas, but organized Lutheran communities were rare. In the 1520s the urban masses were aroused by the spread of Anabaptist doctrines, a radical form of Protestantism which demanded complete separation of church and state. A majority of the Protestant martyrs executed under Charles were Anabaptists. Finally, in the 1540s Calvinism, which had originated in France and Switzerland, gradually spread and grew despite efforts by local and imperial authorities and the Papal Inquisition to suppress it. Philip's efforts to follow the course laid down by his father ended in failure. Calvinism, representing a more complete break with Roman Catholicism than Lutheranism, which retained a good many features of Catholic worship and doctrine, was well organized and disciplined. Whereas Anabaptists belonged to the lower levels of society, Calvinism appealed to educated, wealthy burghers and lower nobility, groups engaged in commerce and finance. Philip undertook vigorous enforcement of the anti-heresy laws and took steps to make the power of the Catholic Church more visible, thereby aggravating the rebellious mood of his Dutch subjects.

In the long costly struggle which followed, religious differences between Calvinists and Philip's insistence on the exclusive position of the Roman Catholic Church were irreconcilable, but they were by no means the only cause of revolt in the Netherlands. Catholics as well as Protestants resented domination by a foreign power and taxation and exploitation of their resources to pay for wars which they did not support and which were indeed in part being fought against them. The upper classes did not want a revolution, but they disliked Philip's policies and methods. The widespread resentment against Spain and the Spanish caused the Calvinists to come out in the open and defy the authority of Philip's government. In 1556, partly because of adverse economic conditions, there were riots, accompanied by looting of churches and monasteries, acts which caused Philip to adopt a more repressive policy. Troops were mobilized from the Spanish armies in the Mediterranean as well as the Netherlands.

The rebels, known as "Calvinist Beggars," gained control of most of the north (modern Holland), while naval units, "Sea Beggars," harassed shipping and troop movements. The south for the most part remained obedient to Philip. Spanish troops won some successes, but these were more than offset by events in 1575 when Spanish soldiers, denied payments because of Philip's dire financial straits, mutinied and sacked the city of Antwerp, at the cost of thousands of lives and great destruction of property. The "Spanish Fury" caused the seventeen northern provinces of the Netherlands to demand autonomy, recognition of the existing religious situation in which Calvinists controlled the north, and withdrawal of Spanish troops. Don Juan, who had been appointed governor of the Netherlands, was forced to make some concessions, but the truce broke down and fighting resumed. But in 1596 it ground to a halt, Philip's financial exigencies forcing a settlement. One of his last decisions, made shortly before his death, was to grant autonomy, though not complete independence, to the Netherlands, but this did not end the struggle. The Dutch fought on for complete independence. Finally in the Peace of Westphalia in 1648, ending the Thirty Years War, fifty years after the death of Philip, the Dutch were granted complete independence while the southern provinces (modern Belgium) remained a Habsburg possession.

While Philip was struggling to hold on to the Netherlands his Invincible Armada had suffered a humiliating defeat by the English in 1588. Relations between Spain and England had been deteriorating for several years. When Mary Tudor, Philip's wife, died in 1558 without a direct heir, the throne passed to her half-sister Elizabeth, whose right was challenged by Catholics. She was the daughter of Henry VIII and Anne Boleyn, for whom he had divorced his first wife. In the eyes of the Church the marriage was invalid and Elizabeth illegitimate. However, good Catholic though he was and though under Elizabeth England was clearly a Protestant state, for a number of years Philip supported her claims because his enemy France was pushing the claims to the throne of Elizabeth's Catholic cousin Mary Stuart. But England did not like the presence of Spanish troops across the English Channel in the Netherlands, and the English were beginning to challenge Spain's control of the wealth in the New World. Their ships began attacking Spanish ports in America and seizing cargoes of bullion bound for Seville as well as attacking payships bound from Spain to the Netherlands. Alarmed over the threat to the bullion route, Philip ordered the seizure of English ships in Spanish harbors in retaliation. Infuriated by this, Elizabeth dispatched a fleet to aid the Dutch rebels and sent another fleet under Sir Francis Drake to attack Santo Domingo and Cartegena in the New World.

Philip then decided upon a direct invasion of England to depose Elizabeth. Elaborate preparations were undertaken and a huge armada of ships was launched. The Spanish viewed the expedition as a holy mission and Philip ordered public and private prayers for its success. From the beginning the undertaking was faced with disappointments and failures; years of planning and huge expenditures ended in catastrophe. Before the expedition actually began Mary Stuart, whose claims to the throne Philip had finally decided to support, was executed in

1585 for treasonable plotting with the Spanish. Once the fleet sailed from Spain, cooperation with the Spanish forces in the Netherlands, a key element in the plan, did not materialize because of interference by small Dutch and English vessels. In a battle in the English Channel the Armada, out-maneuvered by the smaller ships of the English navy, suffered heavy losses. Finally the remnants of the fleet, blown by a storm into the North Sea, made their way back to Spain by sailing around Scotland and Ireland. It is estimated that the Spanish lost forty-five out of sixty-eight ships and about fifteen thousand men.

It was a humiliating defeat, but it did not destroy Spain's naval power. Another fleet was built in a few years and intermittent warfare with England continued. However Spain was weakened, and the enormous cost of the Armada was added to the rest of the debt and financial burden which Philip bequeathed to his successor.

In summary, the reign of Philip, which was remembered in Spanish tradition as the nation's culminating glory, was marked by successes against the Ottoman Turks at Lepanto and a turning point of the struggle against Islam in the western Mediterranean. Portugal was added to the realms of the Spanish crown but only temporarily. It rebelled and was again recognized as independent in 1668. On the negative side, Philip's efforts to suppress the Protestant heresy and preserve the Netherlands as a part of his realm ended in failure as the Protestant north won its independence. Any hopes of subduing England and displacing Elizabeth were shattered by the defeat of the Armada. Under Elizabeth and her successors England became a strongly Protestant country, completely independent from Rome, although the Anglican Church retained similarities to the Roman Catholic Church in doctrine and form. In fact, a result of Philip's efforts was a lasting reaction of intense anti-Catholicism in England. Finally, within a few years England founded colonies in America, successfully challenging Spain's claims to a monopoly of power overseas.

The foreign policies of Charles V and Philip II were not aggressive—their wars were not wars of conquest. Both monarchs were trying to defend and preserve lands which belonged to them by inheritance. Both felt threatened and embattled by outside enemies (the Turks and England) and by internal subversive forces which endangered the religious unity and purity of their realms. There was a consistency of purpose between the Inquisition and their efforts to suppress the Protestant heresy by force in Germany and the Netherlands. Philip even regarded the attempted invasion of England as a defensive move—to check English aid to Dutch rebels and to protect the shipment of bullion, as well as an attempt to buttress Catholicism by restoring the English throne to a member of that faith.

Both Charles and Philip enjoyed only limited success in achieving their ambitious objectives. It was beyond the resources of even the wealthiest realm in Europe to check the forces of change which the two rulers faced, and their concentration on foreign affairs siphoned energy and resources away from the pursuit of a strong unified nation. The result was to dissipate the wealth of Spain and to leave to their successors the burden of a weakened economy and an enormous debt.

Economy and Finance

What were the economic conditions in Spain during the age of Charles V and Philip II? What were the effects of the expansion to the Indies in Spain? Above all, what were the consequences of the influx of precious metals from the New World on the economy? What were the financial and economic consequences of the wars of Charles and Philip for Spain and the Spanish people?

These are questions which have long interested historians, but there is no consensus as to answers. Any kind of detailed examination of them is beyond the scope of this work. We can seek only general answers, and we must recognize that answers are limited by incomplete and sometimes conflicting statistical data and that scholars differ among themselves over interpretation of the data. Moreover we are dealing with a time period of more than a century (about 1469–1598) during which

Spain Under the Early Habsburgs 95

there were many fluctuations. In addition there were important regional differences in a country as large and diverse as Spain.

Seldom in history has a country faced such rapid economic changes as those resulting from the discovery and settlement in the New World and the flow of wealth from the new possessions. At the same time traditional social attitudes and values limited Spain's ability to utilize the wealth in ways which would bring lasting benefits. She was confronted with unprecedented conditions for which past experience did not provide a guide and with which existing institutions were inadequate to deal.

Stories of the New World—of the vast wealth acquired quickly by the *conquistadores* and their followers—led to emigration, usually of young men at their most productive years, which meant a loss of valuable manpower. On the other hand, the growth of settlements in the New World created a demand for the products of Spain, stimulating the economy of the mother country. Demands caused by growing numbers at home also contributed to a short-lived prosperity in the early sixteenth century. The effects were apparent in agriculture, causing lands previously held in common, *baldios,* and some of the land used for sheep to be brought under cultivation to produce needed cereal crops. Some of the wealth from the New World was used to buy tracts of royal land. Land values rose as did rents for tenants. Production increased, not because of improved methods, but simply because more land was under cultivation. But the increase was not sufficient to meet the needs of a growing population at home and in the American colonies, or the demands for food to feed the armies of Charles and Philip. The need for provisions for the armed forces sometimes led to requisitioning of grain from towns where it was needed to feed the local populace. The result was periods of distress and starvation in parts of Spain and the necessity for importation of grain.

The same factors which led to increased demand for food also led to increased demand for manufactured goods, needs which Spanish industry lacked the capacity to meet. Textile, leather, and metallurgical industries existed, but the rate of industrial growth in Spain fell behind the countries to the north. In spite of the influx of wealth from America, Spain had an unfavorable balance of trade. The capital needed for investment in industry was not available. Technological development in general lagged behind that of northern Europe. It is impossible to measure the effect of tradition and social attitudes, but some of the factors already mentioned as deterrents to the rise of a middle class were probably partly responsible for the backwardness of industrial development.

The weaving of textiles was important in a number of cities, in particular Segovia, Toledo, and Cuenca. In Segovia the textile industry began to move away from a domestic system of weaving in the home to a factory system. Growing of silk worms was important among the Morisco population of Granada. Most of the silk was exported to be woven in Italy, but some silk cloth was woven in Spain. However the textile industry, like most manufactures in Spain, tended to be luxury-oriented, not adequate to meet the needs of the domestic market and the colonies. A brief period of prosperity in textiles did not last. Rising prices had the effect of pricing Spanish products out of the market and opening the way for foreign competitors to sell their goods.

That Spain was losing control over its own economic destiny during the second half of the sixteenth century is shown most clearly in the field of foreign trade. The export of raw wool continued to be important to Burgos and the ports in the north. Flanders was the largest market for the wool, while from the Netherlands Spain imported finished textiles, grain, and other products from the Baltic region. The volume of this trade was an important reason for Philip's struggle to hold the Netherlands, but control over it was passing into the hands of merchants and financiers of Antwerp, not Spain.

As the result of the trade with America, Seville, through which all goods were required to pass, was a booming city, visible evidence of the flow of wealth from the New World. As we have seen, some nobles of Seville overcame their prejudice against business sufficiently to invest in the lucrative trade, while others of lesser rank bought titles of nobility with their profits. Nevertheless foreigners came to control a large part of the trade and the profits. This was partly due to the inability of Spanish industries to meet the needs of the colonies. "By its inability to exploit the American market from its own resources Spain condemned itself to becoming an entrepot for foreign merchandise travelling to the Indies" (Kamen, 161). Merchants from all over Europe dominated the business community. Most conspicuous were the Genoese, but persons from other Italian cities, and from France, Flanders, and other countries were part of the international community. Bullion from the New World flowed into Spain, but most of it flowed out again to meet the deficit in the trade balance.

This brings us to the most puzzling question of all—the effects of the colonial gold and silver on the mother country. Until about 1530 nearly all the precious metal coming from America was gold from the Caribbean area. After that silver in larger and larger quantities from Mexico and Peru arrived. The flow reached its peak in the latter part of the sixteenth century, declining thereafter as the best mines were exhausted, necessitating working the less productive ones. Accurate figuring of the amount of bullion which actually reached Spain is impossible. Today it is agreed that the total was less than the fantastic estimates of the seventeenth and eighteenth centuries but far greater than existing reserves in Europe. The relationship between the increase in precious metals and inflation is a matter of controversy. There was inflation—a sharp rise in prices—but the degree to which this was the result of bullion from America is not clear. There were several causes for rising prices—increased demands from population growth in Spain and the needs of the colonies, as well as the increase in precious metals.

At first inflation appears to have had a stimulating effect on Spanish agriculture and industry, but as prices continued to rise, the price of Spanish products encouraged the importation of cheaper foreign goods. Consumers suffered from prolonged inflation; wages rose less rapidly than prices, causing laborers to suffer. Inflation and ever rising taxes were disastrous for many of the poorer classes. In the cities and towns there was a noticeable increase in vagrants and beggars. But the effects of inflation, as is always true, were uneven. Some elements of the population prospered, moving upward in the social scale.

Whatever the relation between bullion from the Indies and inflation, it is clear that Spain did not enjoy lasting benefits from the treasure from its American possessions. Some of the bullion was smuggled out of the country illegally; some of it was captured by English buccaneers in the Caribbean and from the payships sent to the armies in the Netherlands. More important was the failure to invest the wealth from America in productive enterprises in Spain. Efforts of the Spanish government to monopolize the supply of precious metals for Spain were futile. The unfavorable balance of trade forced the government to authorize payment in specie for vital food supplies and other necessities. The greatest remittances were made by the crown itself to pay for overseas commitments—the cost of the army and foreign wars. From Spain the gold and silver from America moved to northern Europe.

This brings us to the question of royal finances under Charles and Philip and the effects of their wars on the development of Spain. As we have seen, each realm in Charles' empire had its own government and administration and each its own system of taxes and revenues, but the costs of his commitments to fighting the Turks in the Mediterranean and Protestant heresy in the north forced him to draw on all parts to pay the costs. To fight the wars he came to rely most heavily on Spain and the Indies. And in Spain it was Castile and the peasants of Castile in particular that bore the greatest burden. In addition to the cost of the military, the most important item in the royal budget, the tremendous expense of building El Escorial and maintaining Philip's lavish and spendthrift court fell upon the Castilians.

Under the terms imposed by the crown the "royal fifth" of the vast amounts of bullion brought to Seville from America went to the monarch. In addition the crown received revenue from taxes on goods brought from the colonies. Large as were the royal fifth and other revenues from America they did not pay the cost of the wars of Charles and even less the cost of Philip's. The cost of the war in the Netherlands regularly required more money than the bullion which the fleets brought across the Atlantic.

In Spain itself there were three main sources of revenue: Aragon, Castile, and the Church. Of these Aragon was least important because of the limited power of the crown in that kingdom where taxes were voted by the *cortes*. In theory the Church was exempt from taxation but because of its great wealth it was considered to have an obligation to contribute to the expenses of the state, especially the cost of wars against infidels and heretics. During the sixteenth century it was under increasing pressure to make regular payments and also extraordinary grants to the state. Tithes, the traditional taxes paid to the church, were not always exclusively for ecclesiastical purposes. For example, Philip received from the Pope the right to part of the revenue to use in his war against the Turks.

Because the power of the crown was greater in Castile, more land lay directly under royal jurisdiction, and most taxes were imposed without the consent of the *cortes*, the people of that kingdom bore the largest burden of paying the costs of the royal establishment and foreign wars. Over three-quarters of royal revenue came from Castile. The system of taxation was complex and also inefficient and inequitable. The most important tax was the *alcabala*, a sales tax or use tax of ten percent originally levied by Ferdinand and Isabella. Because there was no royal machinery to collect the tax, the crown had to rely on the towns and cities to collect the tax and pay the royal treasury. Royal taxes were paid in coin, forcing farmers to find a market for their produce to raise the money to pay them. To facilitate collection and payment some cities received permission to pay a fixed sum annually to the crown instead of collecting taxes on sales. But as inflation lessened the value of money, the value of these fixed payments declined, forcing the crown to seek alternatives. In addition to paying the *alcabala*, towns and cities paid a levy called the *servicio* to the royal treasury. As inflation reduced the value of revenues Philip sharply increased the amounts to be paid. After the defeat of the Armada a new tax, the *millones*, was levied on necessary foodstuffs.

In addition to taxes levied internally the crown collected customs duties on foreign trade, but the revenues collected from all these sources were never sufficient to meet the needs of government, forcing both Charles and Philip to resort to other expedients to raise money—sales of titles of nobility, sales of public offices, and sales of royal land. The last brought in immediate income but limited revenue in the long run because by selling the land the monarch sold the right of taxation to the noble who bought it.

Under both Charles and Philip royal expenditures regularly exceeded revenues, the national debt becoming increasingly less manageable. The deficit increased with each military campaign. Expenses could be met only by large-scale borrowing, mostly from foreign bankers, through the sale of interest paying notes, *juros*. The consequence was that a good part of regular revenues were mortgaged to pay interest. By 1556 it was estimated that 68 percent of the revenue was consumed in this way. Charles borrowed heavily from German and Italian bankers, but as money became more difficult to obtain, interest rates soared from about 17.6 percent in the 1520s to more than 50 percent in the 1550s. All loans were made on the security of the crown of Castile. The increasing hold by foreign bankers on the Spanish treasury led to increasing control of Spain's economy by foreigners.

Philip tried to renegotiate the debts inherited from his father, but confidence in the ability of the crown was shaken and matters for him worsened. He lacked the influence over German Bankers possessed by Charles, and revenues from the Netherlands dried up as military costs increased. Philip's single most expensive undertaking was the expedition of the Armada, but in the long run the war in the Netherlands caused the greatest drain on Spain.

At various times Philip declared a kind of "bankruptcy," suspending interest payments and forcing his creditors to renegotiate the terms of their loans. Although he tried to dissociate himself from foreign bankers, the sack of Antwerp by Spanish mutineers in 1575 forced him to turn to them again to rescue the royal treasury.

The last years of the 1500s were a period of gloom and despair, of crop failures, higher taxes, and deadly epidemics. Gone was the glitter of the "golden century." Philip's reign ended in a perpetual spiral of debt as more and more of each year's revenue had to be committed to payment of interest on debts incurred in past years. Raising taxes no longer produced more revenue—the point of diminishing returns had been reached. In 1596 bankers refused to advance more money, and faced with the worsening financial crisis, Philip had no choice but to agree to autonomy for the Netherlands.

In spite of wealth from the New World Spain remained an economically undeveloped country. One study concludes that Habsburg hegemony in Europe was supported by a two-fold economic base—mining in America and taxation in Castile—and that the latter was more important than the gold and silver from America. Castile remained primarily a rural, agricultural society, the population earning a livelihood by growing crops and herding; hence it was agriculture that bore the burden of the costs of the royal government. It is estimated that at the end of the sixteenth century over half a peasant's harvest went to enrich the non-peasant classes of society, through taxes, rents, tithes, and other payments. "Given that crushing burden in an age of low productivity, it is surprising that the system held up as long as it did.... As long as the Castilian peasant could generate healthy surpluses, the empire could maintain its prestige.... But when agrarian production flagged, the entire edifice began to crumble" (Vassberg, 229).

The Golden Century

The sixteenth century is remembered as the Golden Century (*Siglo de Oro*) in Spanish literature and art. It began at a time when Spaniards were feeling supremely self-confident, when they were winning power and undreamed of wealth from the conquest of the Indies, when Spain was the foremost political and military power in Europe. The phrase *querer es poder* (to will is to do) expressed the spirit of the age. A cultural flowering, coinciding with this period of greatness, continued after the beginning of Spain's economic and political decline. Although affected to a limited extent by external influences, the cultural achievements of the Golden Century were distinctively Spanish, reflecting the Spanish experience.

The reign of Ferdinand and Isabella, bringing stability after a long period of internal turmoil, created an atmosphere which encouraged scholarship. Their reign also coincided with the beginning of one of the most important technological changes of all time—the introduction of the printing press, which was to revolutionize scholarship and literature. Moveable type and the use of paper, which had been introduced earlier, made possible mass production and lower prices for books, thereby stimulating the growth of literacy and a reading public. The exact date of the printing of the first book in Spain is a matter of dispute. (The Guttenburg Bible, the first book in Europe in moveable type, was published in 1456.) It is known that by 1474 a press was operating in Valencia, and it is estimated that by the end of the century some twenty-five presses were in use and that over seven hundred books had been printed.

During the early 1500s Spain was recognized throughout western Europe as an important center of scholarship. The oldest and most famous of Spanish universities, Salamanca, founded in the thirteenth century, had an enrollment of more than six thousand. The founding of numerous universities, endowed and supported in part out of the wealth of the Church, was evidence of the value which the Church placed on scholarship. Most prestigious was the University of Alcalá, founded in 1498 through the efforts of Archbishop Cisneros of Toledo, a stern advocate of the Inquisition, but also interested in establishing a scholarly basis for religious dogma. Under his sponsorship a critical edition of the Bible was authorized. This involved the collection of manuscripts and a variety of texts and bringing together an assembly of scholars who collated the texts. The finished product, the so-called Polyglot Bible, completed in 1517, a great feat in printing as well as scholarship, was printed in the original Hebrew and Greek texts of the Old and New Testaments and in Latin.

Spanish universities were noted for their schools of medicine and law as well as theology. At Salamanca anatomists were allowed to dissect human bodies, a practice generally forbidden as impious. Valladolid was noted for the teaching of surgery. Spanish scientists were pre-eminent in a number of fields, among them astronomy and navigation. At the beginning of the sixteenth century Spain appeared receptive to outside intellectual influences. Cisneros was among the admirers of Erasmus (1524–1583) of Rotterdam in the Netherlands, the scholar who more than anyone symbolized the Humanist movement. A student of the writers of classical antiquity and himself a master of elegant Latin prose, Erasmus loved the Greek and Roman writers because they expressed the ideals of tolerance and humanitarianism which he valued. In addition to promoting studies in classical literature he was interested in religious reform. In *The Praise of Folly*, his best known work, he gently satirized the ceremonial and supernatural aspects of the Roman Catholic Church, urging in their place a religion of simple piety. He was no heretic; in fact much of Protestant zeal offended him. Though Eramus never came to Spain, his writings influenced Spanish scholars. But as Spanish officialdom became concerned over the rise of Lutheranism, his writings, which were somewhat skeptical in tone with emphasis on individualism, became suspect. As Spain became less capable of tolerating new ideas, humanist scholars were silenced and were sometimes brought before the Inquisition.

But while the Inquisition and Index may have had an inhibiting influence, preventing exploration of some fields of scholarship and some subjects in literature, the century was remarkable for its creativity and variety. A reading public, greatly enlarged by the printed press, furnished encouragement for writers of all kinds. There was a remarkable outpouring of fiction, some of it intended to instruct, most of it to entertain. Books of chivalry, filled with stories of superhuman sights and exploits were consumed avidly by readers of all kinds. These *libros de caballerías* remained the most popular form of reading matter throughout the sixteenth century. Even Santa Teresa recalled reading them in her girlhood. Their popularity, regarded as harmful by some groups, led to futile efforts to suppress them in some cities. *Amadis de Gaula*, published in 1508 but based on tales of a much earlier era, was the most popular and influential of these novels. It kept alive the ideals and adventures of the age of chivalry. During the century following its publication at least fifty such romances, running through numerous editions, were published. The *conquistadores* read them. Bernal Díaz recalled that the sight from afar of Tenochtitlan, the Aztec capital, seemed to the Spaniards "like the enchanted things told of in the book of Amadis, and some of our soldiers wondered whether it was not all a dream." California, discovered by a later group of Spanish explorers, was named after an island in another novel of chivalry.

The picaresque novels (a name derived from *pícaro*, a rogue or knave) were a very different kind of fiction, in part a reaction against the excessive romanticism of the novels of chivalry. Though they never enjoyed the popularity of the chivalric tales they were widely read and were an important influence on later European novels. These were stories of low life—about thieves and rascals and prostitutes. The first one, *Lazarillo de Tormes* (1554), was published anonymously, because it even dared to satirize the clergy. By the end of the century the characters in the picaresque novels had become a more realistic picture of Spanish society as the streets of the cities began to be crowded with soldiers—who often had been wounded in the war in the Netherlands—and vagabonds and beggars of all kinds. "Now that the conquests had come to a halt, now that the soldier could no longer find his dream at the end of a gun or spear; now ... it was fitting that the *pícaro* should come to symbolize the defeat of the national dream, and become the embodiment of the national hunger and the national despair" (Crowe, *Spain: The Root and the Flower*, 189). The most popular of all picaresque novels, *Guzman de Alfarache*, published at the end of the century, presented a thoroughly pessimistic picture of society and the world.

The greatest of Spanish novels, and one of the greatest in world literature, *Don Quixote*, was published early in the seventeenth century—the first part in 1605, the second in 1615. The novel in many ways parallels the experiences of the author, Miguel de Cervantes (1547–1616), whose life prepared him for writing the book, the first part of which appeared when he was fifty-six years old. A member of the lesser nobility, always impoverished, he had spent a wandering life. A soldier, he had been wounded at Lepanto and suffered capture and enslavement by the Moors of North Africa. He later served as a commissary for provisioning the Armada. Like Don Quixote he had known many failures but had rebounded from them. His earlier literary efforts had brought few rewards, but the success of *Don Quixote* was instantaneous. It went through numerous printings in Spain and was soon translated into other languages. Before Cervantes had finished his own version of the second part of his novel another writer had written a pseudo *Don Quixote*. A few years after Cervantes' book was published in Spain a play called *The Knight of the Burning Pestle,* an obvious imitation, was being performed in London.

Earlier in his career Cervantes had tried writing for the stage at a time when enthusiasm for the theater was leading to a great outpouring of plays. The origins of Spanish drama are found in the Church and religious observances. In Spain, as in other countries in western Europe during the Middle Ages, spectacles in churches and religious processions were used to illustrate and dramatize religious stories. Out of these came *autos sacramentales,* religious or allegorical plays, presented in churches at Christmas, Easter, Corpus Christi Day, and other Holy Days. For example, to celebrate the presence of Ferdinand and Isabella in Saragossa in 1487, the archbishop of that city staged an *auto* on the nativity of Christ in which persons representing angels, shepherds, the child Jesus, the Virgin Mary, and Joseph appeared. Juan del Encina (1469–1529), who wrote *autos sacramentales,* also began composing dramatic presentations on subjects not drawn from the New Testament but about everyday people, thereby initiating secular theater.

During the sixteenth, and even more in the seventeenth century, hundreds of dramas were written and produced. No other country in any age has ever equalled Spain in the quantity of plays produced. The theater-going public was drawn from all classes of society, creating a kind of equality not found elsewhere, although the upper class always occupied the choice seats. Only two subjects were absolutely prohibited: criticism of Catholic dogma and the monarchy. By far the most prolific of the playwrights, and more than anyone else the creator of the Spanish theater, was Lope de Vega (1562–1635), who wrote more than six hundred full length plays, of which some three hundred survive. Plays did not enjoy long runs; the public was constantly demanding new ones. Most of the plays of Lope and other writers of the period were based on stereotyped themes about stock characters. But in spite of the haste of writing and the superficiality of plots, Lope de Vega was a great writer, an improviser with a vast knowledge of literature and remarkable ability at delineating character. He was idolized by all classes in Madrid.

There were other able dramatists among his contemporaries. Best known today, and the one whose works most influenced the literature of other countries, was Calderon de la Barca (1600–1681), a devout Catholic who wrote many one act religious plays as well as secular drama. His plays, written when the spirit of the Counter Reformation was at its peak, showed a greater concern with theological and philosophical questions and lacked the dramatic impact of de Vega's works.

As might be expected, in architecture and the visual arts the influence of religion was pervasive. Cathedrals, the greatest and most visible evidence of the greatness and power of the church, were usually constructed over a long period of time. Begun in the later Middle Ages, they were symbols of the Reconquest and the emerging Christian unity of Spain. The great cathedral at Burgos was begun and nearly completed in the thirteenth century although finishing touches were not added until later. The one at Toledo, the richest, was begun in 1226 but not completed until 1493; the cathedral at Seville was built between 1402 and 1506 after the Reconquest from the Moors. These were among the most majestic and famous of the more than fifty which adorned Spanish cities. Cathedrals were usually Gothic in style but in details they were a composite of Gothic, Moorish, and Renaissance. The cathedral at Córdoba was built in the midst of the hundreds of richly decorated slender Moorish columns in the interior of the great Islamic mosque. The cathedral at Seville was Gothic, but the tower of the church is a twelfth century minaret from the Islamic mosque.

Most of the great works of Spanish artists were found in cathedrals and other churches and monasteries, some in palaces, but not in art museums. The interiors of the cathedrals, sometimes dazzling, sometimes more somber, contained elaborately carved screens and choir stalls, statues and paintings of saints, and treasuries of sacred objects made of gold and silver and decorated with gems. In the churches elaborate tombs, adorned with effigies, were monuments to royalty and other important persons. Most famous was the mausoleum of Ferdinand and Isabella in the chapel of the cathedral at Granada.

Every monarch contributed to the architectural legacy of Spain. Ferdinand and Isabella, frugal in some respects, contributed lavishly to the building of cathedrals, beginning the construction of those at Salamanca and Segovia and finishing the ones at Seville and Burgos. Nobles and clergy followed their example, contributing to the building and beautification of churches, monasteries, and public buildings. Charles, Holy Roman Emperor, was influenced by the Roman tradition and the Italian Renaissance. The most important example of his tastes was the huge circular Renaissance palace, begun but never completed, within the precincts of the Alhambra at Granada, which he intended for a royal residence. The greatest architectural monument of Philip II, one which seems an expression of his personality, is El Escorial, on the tableland northeast of Madrid, a huge complex of gray granite, at once a royal palace, a monastery, and a tomb. The monastery, begun as an offering of thanks to San Lorenzo for a victory won by the Spanish over the French, was a huge building of long corridors, towers, cloisters, and including a large church. The church was also a monument to Philip's father, Charles V, entombed in a golden mausoleum topped by his statue. Charles was the first monarch to be buried in the Royal Pantheon at Escorial, followed by Philip and most of the later rulers and their spouses. The royal palace, which occupied about a quarter of the monastery, is where Philip chose to spend much time in his later years, and it housed many of his art treasures. His own quarters, however, were simply furnished. His bedroom adjoined the chapel, an arrangement which enabled him to listen to and observe services.

Of the many painters whose works were found in the churches, the most famous and distinctively Spanish was El Greco. El Greco ("the Greek"), whose real name was Doménico Theotocópuli (c. 1548–1614), was born on the island of Crete, studied in Venice under the great Titian, and came to Spain and settled in Toledo about 1577. He did not find favor with Philip II, but his works adorned churches, including the cathedral, throughout the Toledo area. Better than any other artist he expressed the spirit of the Counter Reformation. His paintings of the Christ, the Virgin, the twelve apostles, and other religious figures—with their elongated figures, faces cast upward, and expressive hands—reflect the mystical, spiritual, and somber spirit of Spanish religion. His most famous painting, the Burial of the Count of Orgaz, is a remarkable combination of portraiture of the physical and supernatural.

The realistic, almost photographic style of Velasquez (1599–1660) was very different from that of El Greco. Although he painted religious pictures and some landscapes, he is best known for his portraits. His patron for many years was Philip IV, whom he painted some three dozen times. In his portraits of other members of the royal family and the nobility he left an incomparable record of the royal court and court life in the seventeenth century. Among the younger contemporaries of Velasquez, probably the best known was Esteban Murillo (1598–1663), who painted countless pictures of the Virgin (regarded by some critics as insipid) but also realistic pictures of life among the lower classes—pictures of peasants, street urchins, and other common folk.

CONCLUSION

AFTERMATH AND LEGACY

The period of Spain's ascendancy in Europe was short lived. While achieving and maintaining religious and ethnic unity at home at a great cost, she squandered her wealth and resources on futile wars to prevent religious and political change in northern Europe. The great adventure of conquest in America had failed to enrich her permanently. The wealth and trade of the Indies went in large part to enrich other countries rather than to establish a strong economy in Spain. Having isolated herself from the main intellectual and economic currents of the rest of Europe, Spain, by the seventeenth and eighteenth centuries, had been left behind. Her social system and values were outdated in an age when in the rest of western Europe dynamic forces of commercial and technical change were at work, when there were beginning to be heard demands for constitutional government and religious and intellectual freedom.

The Habsburg successors of Charles V and Philip II, left with a legacy of debt and a weakened economy, were themselves weak and ineffectual, unable to solve the problems which they had inherited or to reestablish the position of Spain in Europe. The last of the Habsburg rulers, the sickly Charles II (Carlos II), having no heir, bequeathed his throne to a distant French relative, the Bourbon who became Philip V, a grandson of Louis XIV of France. The Spain which the Bourbon inherited was exhausted from wars and famine due to crop failures. The population had declined drastically since the reign of Philip II. The death of Charles precipitated another costly war, begun by Spanish dissidents and foreign governments fearful of the increased power of France if a Bourbon sat on the throne of Spain as well as France.

In this chaotic situation of civil and foreign war Philip V and his French advisors moved quickly to establish an absolutist, centralized state. Under the Bourbons the Crown possessed far greater power than under Charles V and Philip II. Bourbons and their ministers, with close ties to the French throne, continued to rule in Spain until the Napoleonic Wars, when they were temporarily displaced. But in 1815 at the Congress of Vienna a Bourbon was restored to the Spanish throne.

During the seventeenth and eighteenth centuries the frontiers of Spanish settlement in America continued to expand. Spaniards, hopeless for the future in their native land, migrated to developing areas in the New World, Argentina in particular. But at the same time the dwindling output of mines in the New World created disillusionment in Spain over the colonial venture, which had become a responsibility rather than the source of wealth and power envisioned earlier. Lacking military and naval power to defend her possessions and interests, Spain saw England and France establishing colonies and challenging her in the western hemisphere. Within her colonies powerful oligarchies of *criollos* developed, with a strong sense of identity and a large degree of independence.

In the late eighteenth century Bourbon rulers introduced reforms which strengthened royal authority, but the Napoleonic Wars again weakened the ability of the mother country to control the colonies and strengthened a movement for complete independence. By the late 1820s wars of independence had overthrown imperial authority in all of the mainland colonies. But although politically independent, the new states retained strong cultural ties to Spain.

The most enduring heritage of the age of Christopher Columbus and the Golden Century in Spain was the Hispanization of much of the western hemisphere. By 1600 Spanish institutions and culture—language, religion, architecture, social customs, and food—and intangible values and attitudes were firmly rooted in the Spanish colonies in America. But, as we have seen, environmental factors and the presence of native populations and cultures created in Spanish America a civilization similar to but not a replica of that in Spain.

WORKS CITED

Collins, Roger, *Early Medieval Spain: Unity in Diversity, 400–1000,* New York: St. Martin's Press, 1983.

Crosby, Alfred W., *The Columbian Exchange: Biological and Cultural Consequences of 1492,* Westport, Connecticut: Greenwood Publishing Company, 1972.

Crowe, John A., *Spain: The Root and the Flower,* New York: Harper and Row, 1975.

Defourneaux, Marcelin, *Daily Life in Spain in the Golden Age,* translated by Newton Branch, Stanford: University of Stanford Press, 1979.

Díaz del Castillo, Bernal, *The Conquest of New Spain,* Baltimore: Penguin Books, 1983.

Elliott, John Huxtable, *Imperial Spain 1469–1716,* New York: New American Library, 1977.

_____, *The Old World and the New, 1492–1560,* Cambridge: Cambridge University Press, 1970.

Kamen, Henry, *Spain 1469–1714: A Society in Conflict,* London and New York: Longman, 1983.

Lynch, John W., *Spain Under the Habsburgs, Vol. 1: Empire and Absolutism 1516–1598,* New York: New York University PRess, 1984.

Payne, Stanley G., *Spanish Catholicism: An Historical Overview,* Madison: University of Wisconsin Press, 1984.

Picon-Salas, Mariano, *Cultural History of Spanish America from Conquest to Independence,* Berkeley: University of California Press, 1968.

Pike, Ruth, *Aristocrats and Traders: Sevillian Society in the Sixteenth Century,* Ithaca: Cornell University Press, 1972.

Todorov, Tzvetan, *The Conquest of America,* translated by Richard Howard, New York: Harper Colophon Books, 1985.

Vassberg, David E., *Land and Society in Golden Age Castile,* Cambridge: Cambridge University Press, 1984.